It's All Your Fault

How to Make It as a Hollywood Assistant

Bill Robinson
and Ceridwen Morris

A Fireside Book
Published by Simon & Schuster
New York   London   Toronto   Sydney   Singapore

FIRESIDE
Rockefeller Center
1230 Avenue of the Americas
New York, NY 10020

FIRESIDE and colophon are registered trademarks
of Simon & Schuster, Inc.

Designed by William Ruoto

Manufactured in the United States of America

10 9 8 7 6 5 4 3 2 1

Library of Congress Cataloging-in-Publication Data
Robinson, Bill
It's all your fault : how to make it as a Hollywood assistant
Bill Robinson and Ceridwen Morris.
p. cm.
"A fireside book."
1. Motion pictures—Vocational guidance—United States.
I. Morris, Ceridwen. II. Title.

PN1995.9.P75 R63 2001
791.43'02'093—dc21   00-0061011

ISBN 0-684-86958-6

Excerpt by Sam Lipsyte reprinted with permission of feedmagazine.com

Praise for *It's All Your Fault*

"Because Bill Robinson was my assistant for two miserable years, you might think I would be enraged to find myself obliquely referred to all over this amazing book. Quite the contrary, I was literally bowled over by the amount of inside knowledge, detailed research, and hilarious anecdotes Ceridwen and Bill offer anyone even remotely interested in a show business career. I laughed, I cried, but mainly I found *It's All Your Fault* a globally terrifying look into the psychology of moviemaking."

—Diane Keaton

"This is the definitive book on the madness of Hollywood. Chock full of brilliant writing, hilarious anecdotes, and above all, juicy gossip. You will laugh so hard you'll embarrass yourself."

—Kristen Johnson, *3rd Rock from the Sun*

"A truly funny, insightful guide about how to succeed in Hollywood. This book is vital for anyone who wants to glean never-before-told insider tips. I only wish I had read this entertaining, smart book when I was starting out—it would have made my early career years so much easier."

—Courtenay Valenti,
Senior VP, Theatrical Productions, Warner Bros.

"From a man who's seen it all, from top to bottom: no better advice can be given by greater experts."

—John Burnham, Executive Vice President and Cohead of
Worldwide Motion Pictures, William Morris Agency

Acknowledgments

The authors would like to thank the following people for their support and encouragement during the inception and endless process of writing this book: Johnny Evans, Courtenay Valenti, Alexandra Valenti, Diane Keaton, Elena Ritchie, Sam Lipsyte, Emily Lenzner, David Brendel, Nora Ephron, Delia Ephron, Jonathan Pecarsky, Sara Bottfeld, Renee Kurtz, John Burnham, Jed Alpert, Erik Arheden, Stephanie Ramsey, Alicia Taylor, and all the Hollywood assistants who remain nameless, hiding and shivering in the dark.

Special thanks to our agent Neeti Madan, and editors Airie Dekidjiev and Marcela Landres for all their hard work.

Contents

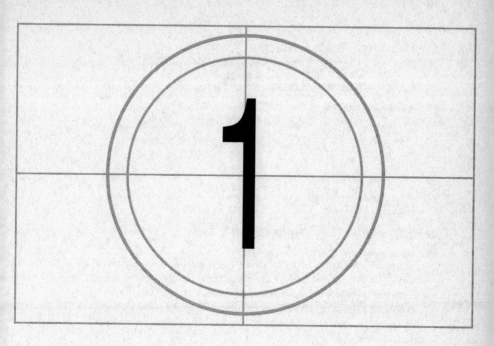

COMING
ATTRACTIONS

The Preview

So go the twisted lives of Hollywood's personal assistants, Sherpas to the climbers of the entertainment peaks, handmaidens to the movie star gods, granters of wishes to the too-rich and too-famous. It might be sushi at 4 A.M. It might be a private plane to Tibet, by tomorrow. It might be exotic animals for a party, or prostitutes for an afternoon. It might just be laundry. But it's always something.

—Washington Post 8/20/98

Whether you're trying to get a foot in the door of the entertainment industry or just love all things Hollywood, this book is for you. The eager neophytes who once flocked to Wall Street are now looking over their shoulders at the life of their friends at agencies, production companies, and studios. Let's face it, it's always been considered hip to be in showbiz and at the turn of the millennium, complete with a robust economy and Internet studio mergers, the biz is booming. Is it any wonder more and more of Generation Y2K wants in on the party?

Starting as an assistant, or in the mail room, is the single proven way to advance quickly in show business. And, for the hordes seduced by the fantasy of Hollywood, it is also the best way to get the closest look at the stars and industry machinations. While it's true many begin life in Hollywood working tech jobs in film or TV (sound, electric, camera, etc.) these tend to limit you to contacts and promotions among technical workers. So if you're searching for broad exposure to the people who call the shots, you're going to want access and proximity to those people . . . access only an assistant job can provide.

Being an assistant to a director, executive, star, producer, agent, or manager can be a great, intense education in how "the business" works. It's like making it through boot camp, and it's hard to predict who will survive. All types live through it and all types leave, including lawyers, film school graduates, and MBAs. This book endeavors to give you the view from under the red carpet. And if you have the sickness required to actually seek gainful employment in the industry, then we hope you will glean the basics in what each job involves and tips on how to succeed, learn as much as possible, and trade up in the food chain of Hollywood. And by "Hollywood" we mean the many cities where the entertainment industry is flourishing, providing the U.S.'s largest exportable product.

Sure, you've seen the images of the peons running across the floor of the stock exchange at dawn. You've seen the footage of sleepless campaign workers giving their all for a candidate. But imagine a similar kind of sacrifice and hard work for the sake of a producer who demands the City of Los Angeles change the timing of traffic signals so that he can have a more "streamlined" drive to work each day. This is a true story, but by no means exceptional in the land that breeds bosses who make assistants blow their noses for them.

The job of the Hollywood assistant is not just about getting coffee at 9 A.M., it's also about getting Forest Whitaker a Quarter Pounder at 3 A.M. There are serious hazards in the workplace as well. Just ask Naomi Campbell's assistant, who got smashed in the head with a cell phone hurled by the leggy beauty during a temper tantrum. One producer cut his assistant's tie off with a pair of scissors because he didn't like it. There's much more to being a Hollywood assistant than just retrieving messages and scheduling meetings, although, as you'll see, the complexity of those tasks alone have led many back to Kansas.

One may assume that the term "assistant" indicates merely a glorified secretary who must perform the usual office duties. However, there is an entire set of rules and special knowledge required to succeed in the highly idiosyncratic entertainment biz. Terminology, geography, and pecking order are just a few of the things they don't teach in film classes.

For example, putting Harvey Weinstein on hold, or xeroxing Steve Zaillian's latest screenplay incorrectly, can cost you your career. Try assuming your boss doesn't mind you giving out his home number. Or perhaps you didn't know that Sharon Stone will never sit sideways to the door of a restaurant. Make just one of these mistakes and you may find out how quickly you can be replaced by one of the thousands of eager young assistant wannabes who are all too happy to work for as little as six bucks an hour.

The first steps you take in this business can be crucial. Reputations are established and contacts made very quickly. If you're the kid who saves the day, instead of the kid who spills the coffee, you may be looking at a bright future. If not . . . you may be used as a target for bottle-throwing practice like one Oscar-winning actress's former assistant.

A word of warning: While you are reading this book you might think, Why would anyone take a job like this? An assistant job is not hell, it's purgatory. It's the rite of passage which, if suffered and surmounted, can land you in those heavenly regions beyond the pearly gates of the Brentwood or Los Feliz estates.

Kathleen Kennedy started out as Steven Spielberg's assistant and moved on to produce hit films, including *Back to the Future, Poltergeist, The Color Purple, Who Framed Roger Rabbit,* and *Gremlins.* Her advice to newcomers is:

> I think a secretarial or assistant position is one of the most valuable positions to be in. In fact, it's unfortunate that most guys

probably feel uncomfortable going in and taking a secretarial job because it's one of the best places to start. If you get in as a secretary or as an assistant to a producer or a director, you're the only person who has access to the entire filmmaking process.

An assistant can be more important and more trusted than a business partner or even a spouse. It's a very intense relationship. It's like a love affair, but a very lopsided one. They love you for taking care of them and you love them because, in a twisted sense, you become them. You must anticipate their every need. You feel happy only when they are happy. You take care of every annoying aspect of your boss's life and enable him or her to do the fun stuff, worry-free. If your boss could have you suffer his indigestion, he would.

There are no secrets between a boss and his assistant. It is a sacred bond, the strength of which we tested when researching this book. Not surprisingly, most of the assistants whom we approached (or who approached us) wished to remain anonymous. What they say often shocks and appalls those unaware of what a sick and crazy world Hollywood is.

The key is to become a jaded industry pro as quickly as possible by benefiting from the hundreds of hours we spent hanging out with Hollywood assistants at L.A. venues such as Capo, Katsu, Ago, Spago, the Ivy, the Whiskey, the Sky Bar, the Dresden, Le Colonial, Cafe Les Deux, Little Door, L'Hermitage, the Chateau Marmont, Bar Marmont, a bungalow at the Chateau Marmont, poolside at the Chateau Marmont, and the parking garage at the Chateau Marmont. And NYC's venerable equivalents: Bubby's, Moomba, Nobu, Match, the Mercer, Ohm, Spy, and Veruka.

The typical evening spent in one of these trendy establishments consists of many overqualified and underpaid entertainment assistants drinking cosmopolitans and martinis next to junior execs who bemoan their heavy workload as they shamelessly schmooze those higher up the food chain in order to gain a job with an even

heavier workload. The assistants, meanwhile, can be found discussing the deals "they" are a part of . . . though this often means
they merely placed the call on which their boss convinced Glenn
Close to do *South Pacific* for television. They tend to share the
dubious attribute of talking only about "the biz" at full volume.
Name-dropping is also common among this junior delta force,
although the same can be said of many of their employers.

But perhaps the most defining characteristic of an assistant
cluster-schmooze is the penchant for trashing one's boss and
complaining about one's quality of life, while simultaneously one-
upping peers with heroic tales of Hollywood insiderness. For
example, one manager's assistant was overheard at an L.A. club
bragging about how he got Willem Dafoe the lead opposite
Madonna in a sexy thriller. When a male star had fallen out of
the project, the assistant took it upon himself to race the script to
the airport and had it flown to Utah, then hand delivered to the
Sundance workshop, where Dafoe was staying. The actor read the
script, agreed to play the part, and the deal was done before
the assistant's boss was back from lunch. Sounds impressive? Not
so fast. The film turned out to be the dreadful bomb *Body of
Evidence,* and, as it turns out, Dafoe's agent had already been
positioning the deal for months.

But the assistant managed to convince himself he now had a
purpose in the cutthroat world of show business and Dafoe
invited him to the set of the film, where he had the pleasure of
meeting Madonna during one of her endless courtroom scenes.
Their meeting was cut short, however, when Sean Penn arrived
and pulled his ex-wife into a trailer for a tête-à-tête. The assistant, left standing in the emptying courtroom, was mistaken for
one of the jurors in the scene and was asked by stage personnel to
return his suit to wardrobe.

The truth is that the above scenario is no less absurd than what
happens to Hollywood assistants every day. Some reassurance:
Many of today's industry success stories, from Mike Ovitz on
down, were kicking copiers and making lunch reservations just

yesterday, so read on. After all, if David Geffen can go from his job as CBS usher to zillionaire and cofounder of DreamWorks, miracles can happen.

The aim of this book is also to show potential assistants:

- how to decide which industry job is right for you
- how to secure that job
- how to do that job well
- how to parlay the job into career advancement

Along the way, we hope you are entertained by the all-too-true adventures of the Hollywood assistant.

Why Should You Listen to Us?

Throwing away his cigarette, he went through the swinging doors of the saloon. There was no back to the building and he found himself in a Paris street. He followed it to its end, coming out in a Romanesque courtyard. He heard voices a short distance away and went toward them. On a lawn of fiber, a group of men and women in riding costume were picnicking. They were eating cardboard food in front of a cellophane waterfall. He started toward them to ask his way, but was stopped by a man who scowled and held up a sign—"Quite, Please, We're Shooting."

—Nathanael West, *The Day of the Locust*

BILL'S STORY

It was Thanksgiving 1990. I was in the house in which I grew up, in Washington, D.C. It had been six months since I had graduated from I-can't-believe-it's-an-Ivy-League Brown University and, like many of you reading this, I had little idea what I wanted to do with my life. All I knew for certain was that I had to get out of D.C. and away from the family real estate business where I had been working since graduation.

I had the usual, mostly worthless bachelor degrees: theater arts, political science . . . but I did have a vague ambition toward the arts. I was the creative type and, like the overprivileged underachiever that I was, I felt a certain sense of entitlement. I didn't want to go to some boring office job sixty hours a week. I didn't want to wear a coat and tie. I didn't want to go to Wall Street or Capitol Hill. Not for me, thanks. I was going to find some way to hang around with groovy creative types and drink red wine and get paid for it. How, you may ask? I had no idea.

Cut to: a well-appointed living room belonging to Jack and Mary Margaret Valenti, whose daughters I consider good friends. I whine to Courtenay, the eldest, who works as an executive at Warner Bros., about not knowing what it is I want to do. Courtenay listens patiently, nodding her head in a concerned fashion, her empathetic gaze clearly the result of her last few studio years spent listening to pitches involving words like "a character-driven dramedy for Steven Seagal."

After telling me how well suited I'd be for gophering in the biz, Courtenay encourages me to think about starting off at an agency, "the nerve centers of Hollywood," she tells me. She'll make some calls, set up some interviews. All I have to do is show up in L.A. with my résumé in hand. It's that simple. Don't worry.

I leave brimming with optimism, so excited about my recently prophesied future that I actually stop at a pay phone on the way home and call Pan Am to make my reservation to La-La Land. "Departure date?" Hmmm, let's see . . . I wanted to do it right. It'll probably take me a week to get an appropriate L.A. wardrobe together (I didn't own any mock turtlenecks or a tuxedo), another week to make some calls and wrap up loose ends at the real estate company, then there's Christmas, then a few days to extricate myself from what will surely be an awful scene with my parents, whose worst nightmare (their son gone Hollywood) is about to come true. . . . "January 2, 1991," spills out of my mouth before I can stop this snowballing fantasy. "Return date?" asks the soon-to-be-out-of-a-job Pan Am reservationist. "Oh . . . leave it open," I respond, sure, in my naïvete, that one day I would say to my Hollywood Hills housekeeper, "Let's frame that silly Pan Am ticket, it was the last time I flew coach."

Cut to Pan Am flight 112, row 78, a middle seat. The scent wafting down the aisle is not glamour, and as the Jurassic DC-10 heaves downward through the smog into the aptly named "L.A. Basin," I brace myself for a heavy dose of L.A. reality. Or L.A. fakery. Whatever.

So what if L.A. is more strip malls than beaches? Or more freeways than palm trees? I had a special feeling about the City of Angels . . . almost what you'd call a premonition. No, not that in a few short years Sandra Bullock would be earning more per picture than Picasso. More like a premonition that good things would happen to me here, and not just because some tourist mistook me for Keanu Reeves at the airport when I arrived.

Now, gentle reader, I know you're thinking that maybe I should have taken it as a bad sign that Pan Am went bankrupt shortly after my flight, rendering my ticket-framing fantasy null and void; or that perhaps I should have become wary when, upon arriving in L.A., the Gulf War broke out, prompting my mother to call every evening to helpfully remind me that I was a "prime, A-1, numero uno draft candidate." But I was determined to stay upbeat as I arrived at the door of an old acquaintance, Roxy, who had eagerly encouraged me to stay with her "in my totally awesome pad." Apparently, "totally awesome pad" translates loosely to "generic, West Hollywood shoe box with stained, gray berber carpet, which you're welcome to sleep on, since there's only one bed and the couch is tiny."

As for Roxy, let's just say I had remembered her as a little wild-eyed and desperate, you know, the unattractive girl who pursues your friendship so aggressively it's just easier to surrender than keep trying to avoid her? Right, that's her. And now that she had me in her clutches, newly arrived in a strange city with no car, job, or friends, and about $300 to my name, she moved in for the kill. Her roommate, it seems, was "like a total psycho" and took off, leaving her carrying a two-bedroom on her own. So now, she told me, I would be paying half of her substantial rent for the honor of sleeping on the floor and listening to sob stories about her endless boy troubles (in which, oddly, they all end up calling her "a stalker") while watching her shovel ungodly amounts of Häagen-Dazs into her yapper. Ah, Hollywood.

But as it turns out, this was a typical Hollywood beginning. Just a few years later, I offered my own shabby sofa to an aspiring actress friend whom I would drive to auditions when we weren't crashing Hollywood parties. I'd like to think it was my lucky sofa that helped Minnie Driver earn an Academy Award nomination for *Good Will Hunting* a couple years later. Regardless, it did guarantee me a date to the Oscars that year. So heed this warning: Pack lightly and carry a big sofa, because in Hollywood, sometimes what goes around, comes around.

Of course, no one had warned me how you really can't get through even one day in L.A. without a car, so I called upon my good friends at Visa to rent me some wheels to do the assistant interview circuit. This was, however, after my first big interview with a studio VP. Wheelless, and assuming Burbank had to be light-years away since it had a different area code, I begged a friend from back East for a lift. Like so many novices, I put on my best suit and polished shoes, adopted the most deferential attitude possible, and proceeded to kiss ass for my allotted fifteen minutes. Of course, I had it all backward, because unlike you, gentle reader, I could find no book on the subject of landing an assistant job in Hollywood. I just remember thinking that I wished someone had written one. Number one: I shouldn't have worn the suit. I mistakenly believed that the movie industry was like a real business, where appropriate attire requirements exist in the workplace. Not so. L.A. casual is the best way to describe the guys and gals I remember seeing running to and from the copier.

Number two: the deferential attitude should have been replaced by the slightly condescending, jaded assistant, don't-worry-I-can-handle-all-your-problems-now-just-sit-back-and-relax-and-take-me-for-granted tone that comprises every executive's wet dreams.

No one was more surprised than I when, halfway through an

interview with the studio VP, she leaned thoughtfully back in her chair and told me that despite my wonderful blah blah blah, and my obvious potential for blah blah blah, she could never work with me simply "on a personal level." Now I was really lost, because I was sure that I could not, in seven minutes, have shown her how truly annoying I can be. "You see," she continued, leaning forward now across the desk, "you remind me too much of my brother who was killed in an accident."

Well, that's what you might call a showstopper. How does one respond to something like that? Seriously. You tell me. Write me. Call me. Collect. Because that scenario haunted me for years after. I mumbled some forgettable condolences and slunk out of the office in such a Twilight Zone state that I just started walking and walking until I saw signs for "Universal City." This, I shrewdly deduced, must be the home of Universal Studios, and since I'm dressed to impress, résumés in hand, why not just head over and improv? Okay, okay, it was a stupid idea, but better you learn from my mistakes than pass judgment on a pathetic twenty-one-year-old in a wool suit schlepping across the San Fernando Valley on foot.

I arrived at the gates of Universal Studios and tried to stand in line between two cars waiting to be cleared on to the lot. I think everyone thought that I believed I was sitting in an invisible car or something, because their glares at me were tinged with just a bit of "Wow, another disciple from the Sean Young school of studio lot crashing." The guard gruffly told me to wait to the side, which I did . . . until I got tired of waiting and just walked, completely unnoticed, into Universal. Important lesson here: Unless you are inside an automobile, you don't exist.

The next lesson I learned, at the reception desk just outside the elevators on the tenth floor of the executive building, is that without an appointment, you don't exist. What did I think I was doing, you ask, showing up blind, armed only with my résumé? No idea. But hey, what did I have to lose?

My pride, it turned out. The receptionist kicked me out. My

college pal Elysa laughed hysterically at how far I had walked, when she pulled up to the Universal Studios multiplex where I spent the rest of the day watching movies in the wonderfully arctic air-conditioning, trying to remember why I was seduced by Hollywood in the first place.

That night at dinner at Mexica—the only Mexican restaurant in L.A. that doesn't serve margaritas—Elysa and another college alum, Michael, sat me down and gave me a crash course on how Hollywood works. Assuming I was dimmer than they had already thought, after hearing the "walk through the valley of death" story, they literally drew diagrams on napkins to show me the connection between producers, agents, studio execs, stars, managers, etc. We will explain these connections later in the book, but for now just know that the napkin had the word "studio" written at the top, with lines indicating studio execs and stars underneath, and then producers, agents, and managers at the bottom.

Michael practically banged his head in frustration as I, idiot that I was, refused to grasp the difference in job description between an executive producer and a studio executive. Now, eight years later, we've just completed a movie together. Michael, now a senior VP at Columbia, served as the studio executive. I served as the executive producer. As Michael said that night, the best way to learn was by doing.

So I started at the bottom, as an assistant to a small-time literary agent. I was treated like a dog and after six months finally was rewarded with a salary raise to five dollars an hour (before taxes).

What transpired in between those eight years serves as the foundation for this little book: A roller-coaster ride working for agents, managers, producers, stars, and directors; my first screenplay sale; a brief stint as a game show champion; a so-called Hollywood success story profile on NBC; the chance to meet most of the greatest living actors in the world; work developing and producing films and television shows for every major studio and most of the networks; several trips to the Academy Awards; a private screening of my movie with the president; and, finally, the beginnings of my own career as a director and producer by way of founding a company with actress-director Diane Keaton.

I remember Courtenay Valenti telling me that there are no rules in show business, no qualifications necessary. I found that a hard concept to swallow, since, like most college grads, my whole life up to that point had been about amassing qualifications. But she was right. And, in the end, I got lucky. But our hope with this book is to prepare others who want to get lucky. Because, as Oprah Winfrey once said, ripping off a line from someone less wealthy, "Luck is preparation meeting opportunity."

CERIDWEN'S STORY

I have no cinematic genes. My family's one questionable link with showbiz involves my father in the early seventies. He was a magazine executive in London and found himself, through a chain of mistaken identities, responding to a *cri de coeur* from Zsa Zsa Gabor. She could not access her jewelry in the vault of a swank London hotel and feared the pricey baubles had been removed by her boyfriend who had vanished with the key. She summoned Chubb, locksmiths to the Queen, all the while clinging to my dad's arm for "protection." Together they led an unsuccessful assault on the hotel vault, which was blocked by the hotel manager and small army of security men. Zsa Zsa then commanded Dad loudly, "Dahling, get me the underworld." My dad headed fast for a cab and that ends my family's link with movieland.

Maybe I always wanted to be in showbiz. My Barbie playing was a deeply involved dramatic exercise. Somehow I fumbled my way through life to the point where I was managing an arts bookstore in Washington, D.C., and curating fabulous underground exhibitions and performances for a small audience of geeks and punks. I was showing cult films by unknown, basement-dwelling, suburban, borderline-personality types and curating "dead-end neoconceptual" art shows about hip things like surveillance and perversion. The gallery was in a great gutted factory, with dirt floors and flocks of endlessly defecating pigeons. I was living the chic life of a pomo, boho art ho. I was happy.

However, you may recall that Washington in the early nineties was not a congenial place for the fringe arts. Newt Gingrich was leading a budget-cutting posse with the Republicans' so-called Contract with America. The arts were not even in the small print. The financial rug had been effectively pulled out from under the NEA, partly (largely?) because the prudes had never really recovered from Mapplethorpe's exhibition. The lingering image of a large, uncircumcised, black dick was too much. Dicks were out in Washington (and have been out, in the real sense, ever since), uncircumcised or not. As my mid-twenties eclipsed the twenty-seven mark, I realized I had to make some real money. I was that person standing in line in some godforsaken check-cashing dump waiting to pay my electric bill.

One weekend I went to visit Alexandra, my best friend of fifteen years, in New York. I had just been dumped by a punk rocker (in his driveway!). On a vindictive whim, I churned out a film treatment entitled *Dumped*, about a girl who gets dumped six times and then gets busted for shoplifting. This venting turned into a serious conversation with Alexandra about writing a screenplay. She persuaded me to give it a shot and we spent the next year commuting back and forth between D.C. and New York.

It was so romantic, reading Syd Field's screenwriter's handbook on the Greyhound, typing into a small, beige Apple. We had no clue how to format a script. We had no clue how to write a script. But nevertheless we staggered on enthusiastically, announcing profound revelations like: "I've got it, each scene has to be driven by conflict." Egged on by the promise of making it big with a spec script, we hammered away. Everyone we knew in Hollywood kept reassuring us: "People out here are morons, the scripts suck, you don't understand, a monkey could write this shit." I didn't want to do something that a monkey could do, but the building my gallery was in was condemned, and despite grow-ing support and a flurry of media attention, the prospect of a little "easy money" didn't sound so bad.

So we sent our script to Bill, someone I'd known on and off since high school. He read it and said, "It's a disaster, I don't even think I know what it's about. But it's hilarious and you should keep writing." Great.

Then he offered to offer me the job as his assistant. Some details had to be ironed out. It was generous of him to offer me the job. He had some serious concerns. I still thought William Morris was a nineteenth-century wallpaper designer. I knew that Courtney Love wore Versace to the Oscars, but I didn't know that forgetting to tell your boss that David E. Kelley called is like for-getting to give a paranoid schizophrenic his medication.

I wanted that job security though and I pleaded with Bill; something about numerous untapped efficiency skills. This was not an easy point. He's known me through all of my sporadic career changes, and unwavering penchant for the non-moneymaking arts, for fifteen years.

So one night, while sealing the return slip for my final unem-ployment check, I received a call from Bill. His assistant puts me through: "I have Bill Robinson for Ceridwen Morris." I consider Bill a friend, but suddenly there's this intermediary, this placer of a call, this person listening in. My future sounds real for the first time: severing relationships, moving to Hollywood, the end of the world, the land of tit jobs and intimidation and crackling cell phone calls placed by assistants.

I quiver on my end of the line, waiting for Bill to tell me whether or not I have the job. Suddenly it's not Bill, that theater guy from high school, it's Bill the producer, never in one place at a time. I am now one of the many things he is doing at once: driv-ing, planning a pitch, responding to a latest draft, looking for the valet parker.

He gets on the line, in and out, apologizing for the "I'm in a canyon" static, when the assistant chimes in, "We've lost him. I'll call you back." *Click.* "We've lost him?" What kind of world am I getting into? The notion that there's someone—an assistant— tracking you at all times, to the point where they know the exact range of cellular phone possibilities, so that they know which call needs to be made when, so that they know, silently on the other end of the line, that I really need this job.

The phone rings.

"I've got Bill Robinson for—"

"Yeah, yeah."

Job offer. I take it.

The morning of my first day of work: Sunshine on my wings, I climb into my fabulously affordable, leased Nissan Sentra. I drive up through the Hollywood Hills, past the many decorator-color garage doors, the Spanish haciendas on stilts, the New Regency split-levels and graffitied aloe vera plants, toward lovely down- town Burbank. The traffic is a smooth sea of sport utility vehicles. I'm wondering if driving to Disney counts as a sport.

The sensation of walking on to the lot is amazing. And I have plenty of time to think about this as my official Disney status had me parked about a mile and half from the offices. As I stroll along the manicured pathways between the peachy-colored buildings, past a theater with a sign reading NO LOOKY LOOS, I actually see squirrels being fed from the hands of healthy, young, multiracial employees. I'm ready for Dick Van Dyke to appear and whip up a quick pastel sidewalk sketch of me in my glorious new dream- land. Messengers wave as they cruise by on their spunky bicycles, even the union workers (snacking beneath a backdrop of seven enormous dwarf sculptures) seem to be riding a seratonin high.

The offices are in one of the legendary old animation build- ings, bungalow style, with breezes wafting through slats between wooden venetian blinds. I am Dorothy. I have arrived. An intern rushes in, looking terrified, like he had just seen someone killed. "There are thirty-four messages and Bill wants you to roll."

I stare at the terrified intern. He stares back.

And then it begins. A weird, seemingly uninterrupted ring. It's a harassing alarm clock blare. Each of the four phones in the room is bleating at slightly different intervals. By the time I've registered the sound, the intern has already answered, and put on hold, five calls.

"Bill, line two." And the kid is gone.

And from then on the day really never let up. I didn't eat, I couldn't, my adrenal glands were pumping me full of superhuman crisis management juices. It was only later when I got home and felt like half a bottle of tequila was the only thing that could bring me down, that I realized, above all else, this town is run on adrenaline. Speed rules. Snatching up scripts before anyone else, dialing half of CAA in under two minutes, pitching two-hour, one-hundred-million-dollar movie ideas in less than five minutes, having yours be the first bouquet to arrive when your client gets a gig. Now, I don't want to get physiological on you. But can the human body process that much adrenaline? What is that gland capable of? I thought it was just there for an emergency. Well, let's just say what lay ahead of me was one year-long, cliff-hanging emergency. And I never left my desk.

I was always on the job. I dreamed Bill dreams. It was like a Cronenberg movie, even my id was not mine. At first I exercised before work, but rapidly I found myself hurtling out of bed, thinking things like, "Drive-on pass, drive-on pass, Nora Ephron needs a drive-on pass," racing to pull on one of my limited selection of appropriate outfits, and hitting the 101 Freeway by seven-thirty. Of course my apartment had nothing in it but a phone and a bed, a fact that didn't really affect me because I was never there.

My happiness was entirely based on the quality of Bill's calls. I lived for a juicy conversation between Bill and his power agent at William Morris. They would get into these huge fights and then make up like a married couple at the end of the day. But for the most part, I would be talking to a fabric cleaner about the exact color of the dog piss stains on Bill's four-thousand-dollar couch, or to a robotic, key-depressing airline employee about every conceivable accommodation in Seattle.

Resentment has wonderful ways of expressing itself. My skills in passive aggression and transference of anger were tuned to perfection. Because I was living Bill's life, I began to make the interns live mine. I soon found myself asking them to buy me cat food and deposit my checks. I had one intern assigned to the task of lying to my creditors.

At first I was very nice to them and asked lots of questions about their goals, but soon I found myself screaming their names, rolling my eyes skeptically over any project they had overseen. It got to the point where I would just throw things at them to get their attention. As Bill used to love to remind me, "It's a dog-eat-dog world and you're wearing Milk Bone underwear."

After nine months as an assistant I had lost a boyfriend (he thought I was secretly "in love with Bill"); I knew two views of L.A.: the one on the way to work and the one on the way home; I basically ceased communicating with the outside world because the only life I knew was Bill's and the assistant bond of confidentiality prevented me from uttering a word.

I was literally speechless.

And then we sold our script, under a pseudonym, to Miramax, with Bill and Diane Keaton to produce. I was the assistant placing calls for my boss in a bidding war over *my* script! And Bill really worked that bidding war. With his help, we not only sold the script but snagged a blind script deal to boot. I owe a lot to Bill for supporting my career as a writer.

So I quit.

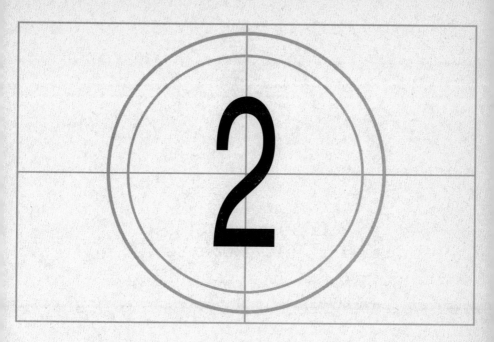

PICKING YOUR
POISON

Assisting a Star: Feeling Julia Roberts's Pain

Everybody wants to be Cary Grant. Even I want to be Cary Grant.
  —Cary Grant

The movie star stuff is fun when you get a good table at a restaurant. That's the only time it works. Other than that, it's actually sad.
  —Sandra Bullock, CBS Online interview

I only hope that we don't lose sight of one thing—that it was all started by a mouse.
  —Walt Disney

So you're sitting in the corner of the Sky Bar at the Mondrian Hotel on the "world famous" Sunset Strip. You've elbowed your way in, past the muscle-head "lister" with the clipboard, by pretending to be some B-list celebrity like Shoshanna Lonstein or Bijou Phillips. Now you sit poolside, charging your vodka gimlets to Freddie Prinze Jr.'s bar tab, unbeknownst to him. And frankly, why bother him, he looks like he's having so much fun with Jennifer

Lopez and Ryan Phillippe on the oversized white furniture. Of course, you can monitor him clearly, since there is no smoke to obstruct your view. After all, this is Los Angeles at the turn of the century, and smoking has been banned in bars and restaurants.

You look around at the throngs of young people in black, smiling so hard their teeth might fall out. You easily identify the different categories of assistants present: those Young Turks talking the most and flashing cell phones undoubtedly work for agencies. They hand out business cards and look overly interested in whomever they're talking to. They're not drinking much, you notice, because they've probably got scripts to drop off at Beverly Hills estates on the way home. That, and they'll be getting up early to make it back to the mail room by 7 A.M.

Next to them, you spot what can only be a director's assistant. He's dressed very casually, jeans and a black T-shirt and he uses his tenuous connection to true Hollywood power to flirt with the most attractive MAWs (Model-Actress-Whatever) in the house. Of course, he's talking about the screenplay he's almost finished writing and how his director-boss is so terribly excited about what little he's read so far, he might make it his next project.

Across the room, you pick out the producer's assistant thanks to her stressed look and the fact that she's actually using her cell phone, furtively trying to deal with some crisis over in the corner. She now scribbles down notes on a cocktail napkin, writing on the back of the actor who would have been her escort home, if it weren't for the assignment she's now receiving via cell phone.

The movie star's assistant walks in, late as usual, to join a table of almost famous people who practically rub his head for good luck. They talk animatedly, someone slipping a screenplay discreetly under the table. The star's assistant greets a few of the minor celebs passing by the table, gently reminding them how they met backstage at Leno and how awful the pastries were.

The sober girl with glasses pays her tab and leaves. She is an assistant at a major studio and she needs to be up bright and early to make sure all the pencils are sharpened with the studio logo pointed in the correct direction. Oh, she's got a few scripts to read, too. Not that anyone will ask her opinion of them.

It dawns on you that you cannot really judge these twenty-somethings at this moment in their lives. After all, the point of being an assistant is to gain the education needed in order to choose the right path. What does it means to work for a movie star, a director, an agent or manager, a producer, or a studio executive? Each have their particulars and each will land you with substantially different credentials.

Before we get into your job description, we need to define the job description of your potential boss. The term "movie star" usually brings to mind Gloria Swanson holed up in some mansion on Sunset Boulevard or perhaps an action star recovering from his latest implant surgery, sunbathing poolside, bikini-clad babes waiting on him. However, stars (both film and TV) tend to be extremely ambitious, highly disciplined professionals, who are more concerned with their protein intake and getting to bed at nine than trashing hotel rooms with supermodels. The point is that no star ever hired an assistant because they wanted someone to share in the good life and to hold the limo door open while they vomit. Of course, there are notable exceptions, which you can research further with the help of the *E! True Hollywood Story*.

For all intents and purposes a major star is essentially a corporation. In fact, almost all stars have loanout companies (tax-sheltered corporations). These corporations, in turn, hire the agent, the lawyer, the manager, the development executive, the trainer, the accountant, the stylist, the driver, the publicist, and of course you, the assistant. The star serves as the CEO of this corporation. Therefore, this modern definition of what it means to be a star is less like that of an isolated diva than that of a Fortune 100 CEO. Chances are that as you read this, Julia Roberts is not curled up on a bearskin rug in front of a cozy Aspen fireplace, but more likely harassing her representatives about why she is only getting twenty million dollars per picture, or going over scripts in development at her production company Shoelace and counting her back-end profits on *Runaway Bride*.

Performing is only one part of the definition of what it is to be a star. To be one of today's fresh-faced ingenues, the modern phenomenon whom we shall refer to as "Gwynona Driver," you have to be well read, well dressed, well spoken, have a great memory, clear eyes, smooth skin, great body, flawless social graces, be politically correct, discreet, and scandal free. Although Gwynona's often photographed at glamorous Hollywood parties, chances are her wine is watered down and she's sealing deals with every air kiss. *Ker-ching, ker-ching!* All work and no play makes people like Gwynona . . . movie stars.

But stars are people, too, sort of, and they know how to have fun. Just be aware that when Tom Cruise dons his life jacket and jumps in the whitewater rapids with such river buddies as DreamWorks founders Jeffrey Katzenberg and David Geffen, it's not about sportsmanship . . . it's about his ambition, his career, his next movie.

To be fair, everybody wants something from a star, whether it's the public, the paparazzi, or even friends and family. To a certain degree, every star lives in a gilded cage. No, we're not suggesting you should feel bad that Gwynona and her male equivalent "Brad Damon" had to stay inside their love nest while a perma-chopper hovered overhead for weeks at a time, but know that if you work for one of these people, you are part of a tiny inner circle meant to protect the star, sometimes even from those closest to him or her.

One final point: there are major differences between a movie star and a TV star. While movie stars tend to be more widely respected, TV stars tend to be more widely recognized. As *3rd Rock* Emmy winner Kristen Johnston put it, "There is no fame like TV fame. If I'm standing next to Meg Ryan at the airport, people are going to come up and talk to me more often than her." Similarly, if Jerry Seinfeld is standing next to Warren Beatty at an airport, more people are going to approach Seinfeld (much to Warren's shock and dismay, probably), because Jerry is in their living room every week and they feel some sort of sick, twisted familiarity. Their viewership entitles them, they think, to the most intimate access and platform to discuss their opinion of every detail of the star's life to his or her face.

One thing you can expect to learn quickly in the Hollywood cult of personality is that fans are losers and that, for the most part, people who approach stars on the street, or ask for their autograph, are desperate people with a rich fantasy life. They tend to have absolutely no common courtesy or sense of boundaries or propriety.

For the assistant, however, fans become a tricky matter since the star knows they must always be treated well, when they are in fact the enemy of living everyday life. You must deal absolutely graciously when responding to fans: most frequently in the form of handling letters and requests for autographed head shots. Stars almost never answer fan mail, a task that is usually handled by an assistant. It is not uncommon for an assistant to forge the star's autograph or even use a stamp with the signature, for correspondence. Better a fake response than no response, after all. Even intrusive phone calls or unwanted script submissions must be deflected with a smile, the same way that studio executives must pretend to like every Robin Williams movie.

Given the perma-smile these high-profile celebrities must affect, unexpressed aggression, insecurity, and moodiness inevitably build into fits of rage, which can be best unleashed on you—the indentured, non-shot-calling assistant.

If you want to be an actor, forget this job. There's nothing actors hate more than aspiring actors. Actors are narcissistic beings and part of their inherent charm lies in their ability to make one feel that they're the only person in the room, so why would they possibly want someone *else* in the room whose aspiration is the same? It tends to get in the way of, well, them. So if you think you have star quality, go rent *All About Eve* and see why the odds are against an actor hiring another actor.

There is no one place in which celebrities find their assistants. Word-of-mouth referral and a discreet, competent personality seem to be the major factors in landing one of these jobs. However, a recommendation by an agent or attorney is the most common way in the dressing room door. In fact, agents will often insert their own assistants into the star client's life, hoping to ensure future loyalty and a pipeline of information. The next best entrée is via the referral of another star's assistant.

And for those of you wondering what it's like to work for Erkel, here is a notable aside regarding child stars: they have guardians rather than assistants, and unless you're over thirty-five or forty, you probably won't make it to the set of the latest Nickelodeon hit series. The guardians may occasionally have assistants, but usually they take care of the embezzlement of some poor child star's salary themselves.

This job can be good for anyone who wants to be an agent, manager, or a producer. Like an agent, you'll have a chance to see how the "talent" thinks and how they like to be treated. You may also be privy to the offers that come in and how those offers are viewed. Obviously, stars want to work on quality scripts with good directors, but the multitude of smaller quirks that stars exhibit when deciding on job offers can be astounding. Some will take a movie role depending on where the film shoots. Others will be more concerned about similarity to parts the star has played before. Still others may judge a project solely on the pedigree of those involved. Sometimes a big star will turn down an expensive movie, because he or she does not want the pressure of having to "open" a movie to huge box office returns.

You'll also be able to read scripts that are submitted to the star, thereby gleaning more information about what kinds of movies or TV shows are getting made. And, if you're fortunate enough to be working for a discerning actor with taste, you might gain from his or her insights into the material. Many actors do not display much discretion when it comes to choosing roles. Some merely take the highest offer. An aspiring producer might want to take note of the specific desires of this or that movie star, because somewhere down the road it might make a difference in landing them for a project.

Whenever possible, go for the actor with a vanity deal (an over-all production deal at a studio that covers the star's overhead and staff). Some infamously rich deals have been made in this arena. For example, former Columbia Studio honcho Barry Josephson made Alicia Silverstone a ten-million-dollar deal that resulted in a one-film oeuvre—the aptly named *Excess Baggage*. Disney shelled out seven figures for Bette Midler's All Girl Productions; Warner Bros. underwrites stars like Mel Gibson and Clint Eastwood, which probably helps pick up the check for less lucrative deals with the likes of Matthew McConaughey and Clint Eastwood's ex-wife Sondra Locke. The latter actually filed suit against Warner Bros. for not taking her overall production deal seriously in the wake of her divorce from Clint. In other words, she felt they were guilty of treating it like a vanity deal. You do the math.

In a way, these kinds of deals are a cynical thing . . . yes, it's about who makes the studio money, but not necessarily in the capacity of a producer. For the most part, it's a payoff. A production deal pays the stars' bills and all they have to do is give the studio a first look at the projects they develop. The studio then has the option to pursue them or not. It is not unheard of for a star with a vanity deal to spend hundreds of thousands, if not millions, of the studio's money and yet never actually produce a single film there. For example, to date Tom Cruise has not made Paramount substantial money through the movies he produces that he does not star in; however, the movies he does star in (like *Mission Impossible* and *The Firm*) make Paramount plenty.

Stars can be notoriously cheap, so a vanity deal can ensure an assistant a higher salary, job security, and probably benefits. While logic might dictate that money is plentiful around this rarified class of artists, many are surprised to find that actors can be stingy with a buck. Often, this is because they are so used to never paying for anything, it would never occur to them to carry cash or do something so "ordinary" as tip the help. On the other hand, many stars don't believe their luck will last and still carry the psychological scars of the struggling actor mentality.

It can also be a healthier arrangement to work for someone who is not paying you directly from their own pocket. Less resentment. After all, you cost them nothing. A deal also means that you will probably get an office on a studio lot, which will give you proximity and exposure to the industry, not just exposure to a star's copious personal needs.

If you want to be an agent/manager, go for the biggest name you can find. Don't cling to your high school drama club opinions about how great certain character actors were in *Sophie's Choice*, because working for them is not going to put you on the fast track. Remember, there is a difference between an actor and a star. By Hollywood standards even James Van Der Beek is a star. Working for a household name gives you instant credibility and leverage. And for you, the Hollywood novice, this is not such a bad thing.

Only the very top box office stars, and even fewer TV stars, get these vanity deals, so if you cannot wrangle one of these few jobs, look for an actor or actress who is on the way up. Generally these types are starting to get a healthy buzz in magazines and on entertainment TV shows, and they are booking small roles but with good directors and in high-profile projects. Pick up the two Hollywood trade papers, *Variety* and *The Hollywood Reporter*, to glean information on who's starting to rise. Look for press releases and scan the production charts in the back of each magazine for casting lists of upcoming films.

A few years back, one young British man had been working as a lowly production assistant in the U.K. when he met up with actor Kevin Spacey. At the time, Kevin was not the well-known star he is today, but the young man eagerly signed on to work for him and moved to California. After the release of *L.A. Confidential* and other well-received Spacey projects, Kevin's Hollywood stock rose and the young Brit, still in his twenties, found himself the producer-partner of one of today's hottest rising stars. Yes, it could happen to you.

Do not get too comfortable, however, with the high-profile glamour of a star's life. The truth is, you will be valuable to him only if you care as much about his horses or pottery collection as you do about his career. He'll remember the care you gave to the job. Actors tend to be sensitive types who will notice everything. Hence, attentiveness, trustworthiness, and discretion are the keys to cash, prizes, and ultimately a promotion. Remember, Madonna's assistant became her manager and Woody Harrelson married his. How? Well, in the first case, by doing a great job in every way. As for the second case . . . ditto.

It never hurts to ingratiate yourself with the loved ones of your actor/boss. Often, insecure actors tend to believe what's repeated to them time and again, and if everyone around them tells them how lucky they are to have "Your Name Here," then they will believe it. If you win his/her trust and support there's no telling how much he/she can do for you. On an intimate level, for example, stars have the power to make dreams come true. For example, after directing his first feature film, Edward Norton rewarded his Bruce Springsteen–obsessed assistant with a guitar autographed by the Boss himself. Norton went to a Springsteen concert in L.A. and solicited Bruce personally. It brings a tear to one's eye, doesn't it?

However, be warned that these types of jobs will not give you broad exposure to all aspects of show business. Instead, you will see the world through your boss's eyes, often a relatively rarefied existence. And, as we've explained, a movie star has to be the impossible dream, so you will be spending a lot of time shopping for gifts, wrapping gifts, delivering gifts, picking up gifts, writing thank-you notes for gifts, and smiling as you receive gifts on your star's behalf. The good news is that many of these gifts will end up at your place of residence. When one star was nominated for a Best Actress Oscar in 1997, her assistant swindled cases of wine and champagne, not to mention literally hundreds of roses, as they poured in from Hollywood "friends." Others have collections of Lalique crystal and endless baskets of bath salts. And it would be hard to find a director's assistant who has not taken home one of the antique movie cameras given from agents and studios "with such thoughtful originality."

A new method of disposing hand-off celebrity gifts is becoming increasingly popular in Hollywood: eBay online auctions. Star paraphernalia is netting hundreds, even thousands on the Web daily. One star's original signed contract for *The Godfather* just sold for $500. And let's not forget Anna Strasberg cashing in on the clothes Marilyn Monroe left in her husband Lee Strasberg's storage locker. Millions were made off of the two dead friends, thanks to an opportunistic widow and an auction filled with creepy collectors. Often the shady auction houses (a redundant term in itself) carry celebrity garb of questionable provenance. Stolen goods have been put on the block more than once. And no one bats a greedy eye. So assistants are thinking twice these days as they clean out Hollywood's garages.

Speaking of garages, you are going to be driving. A lot. And of course, the people who are forced to do the driving are the people least capable of affording a decent ride. Here's one true example we call the "Hot and Silent Treatment."

It's hatchback time on the 405, bumper-to-bumper traffic, 98 degrees, you're crossing the valley on the way back from an antique-clock dealer in Pasadena toward a vet in Bel Air (the only vet "Adelaide likes"). Adelaide—your boss's drooling pit bull whose name has been changed to protect, well, us—is in the backseat destroying what's left of your vinyl interior and the midafternoon sun is a blinding haze in front of you. Your air conditioner doesn't work. Neither does the radio. Hot and silent. Your cell phone rings and your boss wants to roll some calls. Now you really start to sweat. You roll up the window so they can hear you and while zigzagging between lanes, flip through your Filofax for numbers while using L.A. Cellular's three-way calling feature to place calls to fancy offices. Your boss's schedule has just been eaten by Adelaide and he wants to know where and when dinner is. It's a recipe for insanity, not to mention a four-car pileup.

You shuttle like this all day long, sweating like a Tijuana whore and then freezing upon entering one of the many frigid Brentwood environments where you inevitably drop off the usual:

scripts, gifts, antidepressants. This often results in the "Assistant Summer Flu." A common ailment of the assistant with the busted air conditioner.

Not to worry, you'll have plenty of time to rest up when the star boss's upcoming movie bombs. Which brings us to the difference between working for a star on the way up versus one on the way down. Obviously, the former is a more pleasant situation all the way around, but don't be surprised if the oncoming glare of fame and fortune eclipse the once close and humble day-to-day relationship you shared. More success means more people in the star's life and you are now much more expendable. Conversely, the fading star may be much more grateful for the continuing devotion and loyalty of a caretaking figure in his or her life. And never forget that certain laws of physics do apply in Hollywood: What goes up must come down.

Assisting a Director: Lights! Camera! Protein Shake!

It was not so much what the director said, it was the way he said it, especially the way he looked at me (a writer): coolly, confidently, courteously, but with a curious condescension, the way an Englishman looks at an American and an American looks at an Indian. He was a perfectly polite and affable little man and I had the uneasy feeling that instead of standing on my feet looking down at him, I should have been on one knee looking up at him. The man was obviously a prince of the blood. The more directors I met, the more I realized that this was not an isolated case.

—Preston Sturges, from *Preston Sturges on Preston Sturges*

The director/assistant coupling makes for a highly intense one-on-one relationship. Unlike working for an actor, the experience with a director tends to be a much more creative one. The key here is, not all directors are created equal. Often the so-called A-list directors will develop their own material, a process that takes a year or more. The assistant gets to see the script come together (often written in part by the director), the casting of the picture, the negotiating of the deals, the location scouting, the blocking of shots, all the way through to the poster design and the publicity junkets. The most fortunate assistants work for real artists with a singular vision and unique point of view. You know, the Gus Van Sant and Ang Lee group. On the other end of the spectrum there are the hired hacks: directors who come on board in the final hour to scream "Action!" Many an Adam Sandler movie is made this way.

The bottom line is some directors have vision, some don't. How can you differentiate? A simple rule: Always judge a director by his or her work. It's no good to say, "Oh, well, the script was poorly written," or, "The acting sucked," a director is responsible for everything down to the color of a doorknob. If a movie doesn't work, it's generally the director's fault.

Starting out in Hollywood, you will hear how directors are abused and sabotaged; how overly strident producers or studio execs muscle them into compromises they didn't want to make. Or you'll hear about how the studio got final cut and the director had a great movie until the studio yanked it out from under him. Unfortunately, all this does happen in the moviemaking process. But ultimately, a director is responsible for the people, projects, and contracts with which he is associated.

When a feature director signs on to a picture, he basically has to acquire tunnel vision for at least a year. All that exists is that movie. And that goes for the assistant, too. You'd better hope you like this movie, so try not to get stuck assisting the director of *Jungle to Jungle* unless you want to spend your time dreaming about Tim Allen's mosquito allergies.

And it can get a lot worse than that. Take the story of one of Hollywood's top assistant directors, K. C. Colwell, who went into the thick of the Amazon to work on an action picture. One scene required dozens of killer snakes threatening the characters on a small boat in the middle of the river. Of course, only a few of the many snakes were real, the rest were snake puppets that required human hands to effect their realistic movement. Problems arose, however, when the unprepared animal handlers realized that (surprise!) they did not have any English-speaking volunteers with free hands while the cameras were rolling on a boat in the middle of the river in the Amazon. So K.C., along with the director and producer, had to squat in the corners of the boat and operate the snake puppets. The handlers assured K.C. that the actual anacondas would not attack unless threatened and that they would move toward any small, dark area they could nest in. This all seemed okay, given the hellish circumstances, until the director called "action!" and one of the real, deadly anacondas started for K.C. He looked down to see the baggy legs of his shorts hanging down and the anaconda slowly raising its head to peer into the tunnel this created underneath his leg. K.C., usually a brave kind of fellow, held his breath and tried not to yell out while the camera was rolling, knowing that if he did, they would all have to go through this again for take two. Thankfully, the snake decided against entering K.C.'s shorts and lowered itself onto the floor of the boat just in time for the director to yell "cut!"

So why is working with a director such a brass-ring job? One must appreciate what it means to act as the director's right hand. Not only are you able to read and help find material, but you are also involved in all aspects of making a movie from beginning to end. Whether it's sitting in casting sessions or traveling to exotic locations, the director's assistant is allowed the ultimate backstage pass to moviemaking.

Often, a director will have more than one assistant, though generally only one assistant really "lives" with the director on set, in the car or van, on the plane, etc. And, for most eager young assistants, on the set is where you want to be. Or so you think.

The whole "being on set" notion is so overly romanticized that one is bound to be disappointed, no matter what the project. Even most tourists who visit studio stages during filming, their purses strapped on canteen-style, become bored after an hour of watching virtually nothing happen. They might catch some reaction shot of a bunch of extras pretending to laugh at Steve Martin's "crazy antics" shot two weeks ago against a bluescreen.

The overwhelming boredom one feels on a set is made worse by the occasional bouts of intense off-camera drama. There is always a problem, personal or production-oriented. And the director usually ends up involved in whatever's rocking the boat. Whether it's the star's new haircut that doesn't match the first half of the scene shot yesterday or the Thai government's attempts to deport Jodie Foster's *Anna and the King* crew, there is rarely a "normal" day of production on a movie.

The phrase "hurry up and wait" is often associated with the filmmaking process and for good reason. One assistant to director Oliver Stone would try in vain to get answers to pressing questions. She couldn't reach him for days. Then one morning the phone rang at dawn with an irate Mr. Stone demanding, out of the blue, "Where the hell are my helicopters?!"

No matter what the scale of the picture, assisting a director demands that one become as much of a spin doctor as George Stephanopoulos. You answer questions for your boss, you deflect others. You disseminate reams of information to department heads and production staff and serve as a conduit to the director. You try to take credit and pass blame, though you will receive all blame and no credit.

Of course, there are tremendous advantages to working on the set. In addition to learning about the filmmaking process, you can be appreciated by many people. You can develop more relationships than if you are confined to an office all day and you'll learn how to behave on the set. We will refer to this behavior as "setiquette." Here are the ten primary rules of setiquette:

1. Don't speak unless spoken to.
2. Knock loudly on trailer doors before entering.
3. Never talk to nosy neighbors on location.
4. Never criticize the food.
5. Don't offer opinions on script, performances, or direction.
6. Don't sit down unless invited.
7. Never walk on to a "hot" set (i.e., one being used that day).
8. Never ask for haircuts or makeup.
9. Don't predict how the project will do.
10. Never ask for autographs.

The director's assistant has to be a diplomat, a messenger, and extremely sensitive to the politics of every situation. The set can be a crazy place where emotions and egos run high. Every word must be watched.

A typical example occurred during the shooting of a young director's brilliant debut. A major diva was cast opposite a male newcomer. The latter was said to have taken himself quite seriously as an actor and even went so far as to compare himself to Marlon Brando. The diva, a close friend and former lover of Brando's, went ballistic. She gave the newcomer the "I know Marlon Brando, and you're no Marlon Brando" speech and then shooting came to a standstill. No one would apologize, naturally. Who do you think had to take it upon himself to patch up that insanity? That's right, the fledgling director.

Obviously, working for a seasoned director can be easier and less dramatic in many ways. But it has its tradeoffs. Yes, you want to be Scorsese's assistant, but if you want maximum set exposure, work for someone like Brett Ratner, who serves up the finest Charlie Sheen and Jackie Chan have to offer.

One of the most advantageous routes you can take these days is to get in good with a hot commercial or video director. Some of the best-known examples of their huge crossover potential are Michael Bay *(Armageddon; The Rock; Con Air)* and Simon West, who directed those Budweiser frog commercials on his way to an equally compelling *The General's Daughter*.

These types of directors serve up a dazzling visual style with glee. And although their stories often leave much to be desired, that's not to say their assistants will only learn the art of cheese. For example, commercial director David Fincher, who went on to direct *Seven, The Game,* and *Fight Club,* hired an assistant named Claudia Sachs, who, as she put it, "had mixed feelings working on *Alien 3.*" But she parlayed her experience into a vice presidency at Spyglass Entertainment, where she worked with some of the best writers and directors in the business.

Indeed, Bill got his break as Diane Keaton's assistant when she

signed on to direct *Unstrung Heroes* for Disney. For almost a year
before shooting, Diane let Bill work on the script with her, a
process they repeated when Keaton starred in *Amelia Earhart*.
Without a doubt this helped Bill to sell his first screenplay to
Disney later that year.

Some assistant stories don't have such a happy ending, however. Renny Harlin got involved with an assistant on an international publicity tour; she later had his baby and went to court over
child support.

On a lighter note, many director's assistants really get a
chance to enjoy themselves during the casting process.
Opportunities exist to meet hordes of famous faces and to
watch them sweat while trying to land a role. One of our
favorites involved Bill's "reading" opposite actors for the lead in
a Warner Bros./Steven Spielberg project called *Pet People*. The
role called for a star who could play a family dog who magically
turns into a man one day. During the screen tests, Bill was
assigned the inelegant task of making the actors do dog tricks.
While everyone involved felt rather uncomfortable about the
twenty-four-year-old assistant telling A-list stars to "sit" and
"beg" and "roll over," it was heartthrob Antonio Banderas who
really pushed the situation to the extreme. He asked Bill to tear
up pieces of bagels from the craft services table and throw them
for Antonio to catch in his mouth, while scrambling around on
the ground on all fours. Bill obliged, even having Antonio beg
and whine while perched on his haunches nipping at Bill's fin-
gertips for the bagel bits. Despite his barking and, literally, begging, unfortunately Warner Bros. did not feel Antonio was the
pick of the litter. He didn't get the part, and to this day Bill
blames himself.

As you might expect, directors can be difficult people. Most
of them are men and most are used to having their every word
obeyed unquestioningly. Naturally, this can adversely affect
their humanity and the personal relationships directors have
with their assistants can be very dictatorial. Yes, there are

increasing numbers of female directors, but gender does not necessarily dictate humility. If you think Penny Marshall or Jodie Foster got where they are by being nice, you are sadly mistaken.

Assisting an Agent or Manager: How to be Satan's Handmaiden

I'll do anything for money—even associate with my agent.
—Vincent Price

So you want to work in a hostile, tense, fluorescently lit environment with long hours and low pay? Have we got a job for you! As an assistant to an agent or manager you will be in the nerve center of the biz: the deal making, the scripts, the thousands of phone calls to everyone in a 310 or 212 area code.

There are currently five major agencies: William Morris, ICM (International Creative Management), Endeavor, CAA (Creative Artists Agency), and UTA (United Talent Agency). They like to think of themselves as these vastly different and individual companies, which is somewhat akin to pondering the wildly divergent flavors of 7UP and Sprite. For the most part, they are the same company; many agents have worked for more than one of these agencies and they, as well as the clients, continually shuffle back and forth. Some of CAA's senior agents defected from William Morris; Endeavor was founded by renegade ICM agents who stole office files in the middle of the night; William Morris and

UTA have absorbed smaller agencies to stay vital. And William Morris's top positions are presently held by former ICM agents.

The perceived differences between the companies come down to this: William Morris is old, rich, and claims supremacy in TV packaging based on relics like *The Cosby Show;* ICM consists of top agents who compete with one another and run separate fiefdoms; CAA uses Mafia tactics to intimidate clients in a gorgeous I. M. Pei building they rent from their mortal enemy, Michael Ovitz; UTA is young, aggressive, and sometimes mistaken for a personal injury law firm; Endeavor is rapidly growing and turning into CAA, by signing clients with the line, "We're a small company, the opposite of CAA."

These differences should not mean much to the aspiring assistant. The only thing that matters is working for the agent with the best client list and the most clout. And now that many top stars like Jim Carrey, Brad Pitt, Robin Williams, and Helen Hunt have both agents and managers, the neophyte assistant may also opt to work for a manager in order to gain similar experience.

First, let's start by clarifying the difference between an agent and a manager. Technically an agent is bonded with the state and has the right to procure and negotiate work for a client (actors, writers, directors, composers, etc.). A manager, not bonded with the state, is technically not allowed to procure or negotiate work for a client. Instead, they are supposed to help clients make advantageous career choices, as well as handle much of the minutiae of a client's life.

Agents generally receive a 10 percent commission, managers often get 15 percent. Sound a bit skewed? Wait, it gets worse. Managers are also allowed to produce their client's work or the work of others. Agents are forbidden to produce. This would be so-called double dipping: that is, commissioning a client and then taking a producing credit and fee on some of the client's work. The fact that managers are perceived as double dippers is increasingly becoming the subject of litigation, media speculation, and tremendous uproar in Hollywood. As of the writing of this book,

once-upon-a-time superagent Michael Ovitz is forming a company AMG (Artists Management Group) that hopes to manage,
produce, and even distribute clients' work. With clients such as
Leonardo DiCaprio, Cameron Diaz, Robin Williams, Sydney
Pollack, Barry Levinson, and Martin Scorsese, is it any wonder
many in the industry are calling this a monopoly?

One recent example of how this conflict can explode came in
1998, when Garry Shandling filed a one-hundred-million-dollar
suit against his former manager/producer Brad Grey of Brillstein-
Grey. His manager, Shandling contended, had a conflict of interest and used Shandling's successful *Larry Sanders Show* to leverage
a rich TV deal for himself. Grey paraded a list of TV executives
who swore affidavits that his deal didn't have to do with
Shandling. The suit was eventually settled out of court before trial,
but the impression of a conflict of interest remains in the minds of
many. In fact, there is now legislation pending in the California
state legislature that would regulate managers.

There are two very divergent opinions on managers. The positive view is that managers serve to fill a critical gap in servicing
clients who are, for the most part, represented at big agencies that
function more like faceless corporations than personal service
caretakers. While agents bring in the scripts and offers, a manager sees his job as helping the client sift through it all and make
the best possible choices. "Overall career strategy" is a phrase
you'll hear at least once an hour at any management company.

When Bill worked for a top Hollywood manager, she had a
favorite line she'd use on prospective clients when they'd ask, "So,
like, why do I need to pay both an agent and a manager? What
does a manager, you know, do, exactly?" "Darling," she'd reply, "we
do everything you wish your agent would, but doesn't." The idea
being that managers, because they tend to have far fewer clients
than agents, pay closer attention to all aspects of the talent's
career and life. For example, that same manager had a now infamous mother-daughter-type relationship with the young Melanie
Griffith, whom, she told *Vanity Fair*, she rediscovered, made over,

bathed, sheltered, advised, promoted, and built into a star. After the manager moved heaven and earth to get her cast in *Working Girl*, for which Melanie was nominated for an Oscar, she came home to a cold note on her door informing her that Melanie would be terminating their relationship. Melanie, for her part, recalls the experience thus: "She made a few phone calls for which she was paid handsomely."

This brings us to the negative take on managers. Like agents, they can be viewed as a necessary evil; parasites who live off of talent, taking their percentage in exchange for "protection," not unlike the mob. The world of management, at its worst, might be seen as "a long, plastic hallway where pimps and thieves run free and weak men die like dogs." One top actor, in the process of being courted by Ovitz's new management company, said, "My feeling is that managers really promote the idea of artist as idiot. As morons not able to think for themselves. They need to cultivate this idea for their own survival. They feed off of it." Indeed, director Sydney Pollack, when faced with having to choose between CAA or AMG in their bitter feud, responded with anger, saying, "You guys have it backwards, you're making yourselves the star here. . . . I pay you a lot of money to protect my interests and now you're telling me who I can and cannot talk to?"

As you can see, the management field is one of the most controversial areas of the entertainment business right now, but also the most exciting and potentially expansive, the L.A. version of Internet stocks. Agencies, on the other hand, tend to be a less dramatic way to go. Generally speaking, they are larger, more bureaucratic, and, unlike managers, legally regulated in a way that limits cowboy behavior. An agency will also take longer to promote assistants, but, unlike most management companies, the larger firms have trainee programs specifically designed to serve as a kind of grad school.

This job is best suited for those interested in becoming their agent/manager boss or a producer, because it puts you in proximity to scripts, talent, and the buyers at studios and networks.

However, it tends to be a waste of time for aspiring actors or writers . . . after all, no one is eager to represent the guy who knows all about his drug habit. The upside of an agency job is that they will commit if you will commit. In other words, if you take the "trainee" route and start in the mail room, within two to three years you stand a good chance of becoming a full-fledged agent.

The difference between talent agents and literary agents can define the preferred path for different personality types; personalities, which, in all cases, must be able to cope with insanity, abuse, and manic depression. Talent agents tend to have a more solicitous, smothering nature. They are often gay men or overweight women—or both. They are usually bitter, as they watch people they discovered achieve fame and fortune only to dump them for a more powerful agent. One of the most successful agents of all time, Sue Mengers, was so destroyed after losing her most treasured client, Barbra Streisand, that she ended up leaving the business and now rarely leaves her house.

Literary agents often affect a smug, erudite manner, because they occasionally read books (well, at least the coverage). They represent directors ("filmmakers" is now the preferred vernacular) and they don't have to do the full-on Hollywood scene to be successful. Let's face it, who even knows the name of Stephen King's agent? But this doesn't mean lit agents are any better to work for than talent agents. It is true that one prominent literary agent beat his assistant over the head with a rolled-up copy of *Variety* because the assistant put staples "at the wrong angle" on various documents.

There is also the story of a well-known ICM agent who, while dining on the patio at the Ivy in Beverly Hills with Johnny Depp, Kate Moss, and other skinny people, demanded that the heat lamp be moved away from their table. When she was informed that it was cemented into the ground, she threw a fit that resulted in several employees being reprimanded "for their incompetence."

Perhaps the hardest part about working as an assistant to an agent or manager is not only the responsibility of keeping track of your boss's schedule, calls, meetings, meals, etc., but also keeping track of your boss's clients' schedules, while maintaining a people-pleasing demeanor that would impress even the world's best stewardess. The number one priority for the agent or manager is to keep the client happy. This means that you might have to call that flaky writer or that drug-addled actor the week before, the day before, the hour before his next meeting. Then you have to tell him who it's with, what it's about, and give him directions. All the while you must continue juggling your boss's agenda, which, whether he/she is successful or not, will be crammed full of schmooze sessions separated by rapid-fire meetings. You've seen it in the movies: "Get me my agent!!" The agent is the link to everyone's next job, so these assistants are mostly dealing with extremely worried people.

Often, the agents themselves can be eager on the phone. As an assistant, there will be no end to the drama of the telephone when it comes to placing calls. A typical example can be found in the true tale of major UTA agent, Traci Jacobs, who was rather eager to get a certain producer on the phone. When he would not take her call, things heated up. As the producer himself said, "It was extraordinary. My assistant called out, 'Traci Jacobs on line one.' Then, two seconds later, I heard, 'Traci Jacobs on line two.' Then, 'Traci Jacobs on line three.' A moment later, 'Traci Jacobs on line four.' Then, my cell phone rang. Guess who?"

There is undoubtedly something truly hilarious about the ways in which the denizens of Hollywood torture one another. And this holds true for assistants as well. The passive-aggressive tactics that assistants use against their agent-bosses can be quite sly. For example, a top William Morris agent was continually obsessing over his weight and was almost always on a diet. Whenever he would have large meetings in his office, his assistant would be sure to order lots of food (entrées on separate plates) and as staff members arrived for the meeting, the assistant would politely ask them to bring in course after course of heaping plates for the agent. Those in the meeting would gasp in amazement as the plates would pile up in front of the oblivious agent as he grazed unconsciously.

But of all the absurdity, as an assistant to an agent you will find nothing more ridiculous than the unsolicited screenplays that are sent your way. Although most assistants know better than to read unsolicited material, we met one who just couldn't resist taking a peek at *Goodfeathers*. Yes, it's true, he had been asked to give his big shot boss this script "about a parrot who witnesses a Mafia murder and must go into the witness protection program." The kicker? The parrot only spoke in Spanish, so subtitles were required. And, *Goodfeathers*, it turned out, was a drama. We wish we could say this was an exceptional situation. Sadly, there are *Goodfeathers* everywhere in Hollywood.

Speaking of drama, one manager's assistant we know had the unenviable assignment of rushing to the set of a B movie in Hollywood to try and pry a drugged-up movie star out of his trailer. The star, though fairly young, was already on the decline due to self-destructive behavior and a failed marriage to a top starlet. After barely passing the physical and drug tests necessary for the film to be insured, the actor had now barricaded himself in his trailer, while the producers demanded to check between his toes for needle marks. The hapless young assistant helped the manager and producers gain entry, but that was only the beginning of the end. The actor stopped working, the film shut down, and the manager was sued for the behavior of the client. The assistant was dragged into the mess, ultimately swearing out an affidavit about the debacle.

To end with yet another cliché, "If you lie down with dogs, you wake up with fleas." Well, most agents and managers are not really dogs, though they are required to do some of the most ferocious barking in Hollywood. But as an assistant in this arena, you should expect a certain amount of emotional, and possibly physical, scarring.

Assisting a Producer: The Best of Times, the Worst of Times

The pain of having to collaborate with such dullards and to submit myself to their approvals was always acute. Years of experience failed to help. I never became reconciled to taking literary orders from them. I often prepared myself for a producer conference by swallowing two sleeping pills in advance.

—Ben Hecht, *A Child of the Century*

It's 5 A.M. in a New York hotel suite. Day thirty-five of shooting. The producer is in the shower while his assistant sits at the bathroom vanity rolling calls. Naturally, no one in NYC or L.A. will answer the phone, which is just how the producer likes it. He will call the people he actually needs to speak with later. For now, he will "dump" the calls that he does not stand to gain anything from. But should some writer or director or agent actually be there to answer the phone, the producer will hop out of the shower and honor the call he's placed, taking a sick pleasure in the brilliance of his scheme. After all, he's returning everyone's call, so isn't he polite? This sociopath producer mistakenly assumes the sheer hostility of returning a call at 5 A.M. will be overlooked by the people to whom he is doing this great courtesy.

In the meantime, he shouts a list of things he needs done from the shower to the assistant. Flowers sent, scripts fetched, faxes fired off, story notes dictated. All this before the Towncar picks him up at 5:30 A.M. sharp to take him to the set, the assistant still handcuffed to him. Once on set, the producer will continue the multitasking, alternating calls for other projects with the necessary intrusions into the movie being made in front of him.

He is a combination of shrewd businessman, savvy diplomat, creative visionary, and whip-cracking taskmaster. He has to understand story, the marketplace, and how to work with agents, executives, directors, writers, and "talent."

In Hollywood, many people want to produce, but to really succeed in this field it takes da Vinci–like versatility. Not to mention fierce determination and the patience to push a project relentlessly, for what often amounts to years and years. Ever wondered why the Best Picture Oscar goes to the producer? Because usually the producer has been with the movie the longest: he takes the product, often supplied by the agents, packages it (with writers, and/or a director and star) and sells it to the studio (usually the studio has acquired the script rights before official offers are made).

He then shepherds the project through the system on the way to making a movie, from the initial concept or script, to the planning of a shooting schedule and budget, the location scouting, the casting, all the way through to the final scoring session. And then, even after the film is "in the can," there are still test screenings, marketing, domestic distribution, and eventually international, video, cable, and network television sales.

A producer can have a deal with a studio whereby the studio pays for his overhead and staff in exchange for having a "first look" at anything that producer intends to make. This is a swank deal, desired by all producers because it gives a production company the time and money to develop projects that may or may not be bankrolled by the studio with which they have a deal. Of course, it makes sense for the producer with a studio deal to make a movie at that studio in order to prolong a lavish lifestyle afforded by the excessive use of studio dollars.

Back in the Golden Era, producers were hired executives at studios who were most often assigned a picture, complete with script, cast, even crew. The modern producer is technically independent of the studio and must sell his or her product to the studio or to a financier. You will quickly learn that a "financier" is basically anyone who will invest money in a film, hoping for a disproportionate return. This includes arms dealers, Swiss insurance companies, Middle Eastern royalty, eccentric Texas millionaires, and junk bond dealers. Television movies are often sponsored by huge conglomerates, like Johnson & Johnson or Kraft or Hallmark. These corporations know that it is worth their while to underwrite two hours of CBS Sunday night programming. After all, it doesn't take a genius to figure out that anyone who enjoys *Touched by an Angel* is going to love aerosol cheese.

One of the most commonly asked questions about producers concerns the amount and variety of producing credits. For example, a studio representative can don the title "executive producer" (take Miramax's Harvey and Bob Weinstein, for example) though they are usually not involved to the extent of the "hands-on" producer, who is the one in the day-to-day trenches.

Writers can sometimes leverage the title "executive producer" on movies they write. This can be a payoff for the more successful writers and it's also a way for them to guarantee that they will not be thrown off a project. Studios will sometimes prefer to give a writer the credit instead of a higher paycheck. Executive producer/writers also have a voice in the making of the movie. Many writers try to obtain this but few succeed. Only big shots like Ron Bass *(Stepmom)* or Joe Eszterhas *(Basic Instinct)* are in the running.

Movie stars can extort executive producing credits relatively easily, if they act in a TV movie or series. Glenn Close, Meryl Streep, and Sarah Jessica Parker are some recent examples. Film producing credits are more difficult to obtain, although that didn't stop one young actress from a four-year quest to secure herself the title of "producer" on a project set up by two producers at New Line.

Although the young woman in question was the most famous actress under the age of twenty-five, the producers wanted Juliette Lewis for the role instead. But Juliette was in seclusion on an ashram, so the producers hired the less-talented famous actress, who, at the time, was found on the cover of every magazine. After all the contracts were negotiated, the starlet slipped in a last-minute demand for her assistant to have the modest role of associate producer on the film. Although it seemed an oddly inappropriate request, everyone acquiesced to placate the starlet, who, in the midst of the deal, had fired her agent.

About a year later, when it became clear that New Line would not make the film, the original two producers moved the project to Twentieth Century Fox, with the actress still attached. The starlet now demanded her new partner (a bright young woman) be entitled to a credit as executive producer of the film. Once again taken aback, the producers and studio acquiesced in an effort to placate the unstable young actress, who, once again, fired her most recent agent in the midst of the negotiations. But it didn't stop there.

When the studio finally wanted to start production on the film, the twenty-something diva, who may or may not have graduated high school, brought the project to a screeching halt when she hit the producers and studio with the ultimatum that her newly formed production company should also get a credit at the beginning of the movie. Well, although everyone once again acquiesced to the starlet's demands, this turned out to be the straw that broke the camel's back. The project went south and the studio bought the exact same true story from a different film-maker with a different lead actress who went on to win an Academy Award for playing the role.

The title "associate producer" is often simply a vanity credit or a bargaining tool to limit someone's involvement in a project, as in,

"We'll give him associate producer credit to make him go away." It's a credit that usually comes at the end of the movie, buried in the technical credits. Associate producers are not accorded most perks belonging to full-fledged producers, their names do not appear on the budgets, on daily shooting schedules, or other official documents. The associate producer's name is less likely to appear after the words "Dear____" or "Attention:_____" and more likely to appear after "cc:_____." This credit can go to the young, unknown person who does all the grunt work that a producer should do. But he accepts the credit of associate producer because he simply doesn't have the contractual precedent of a fancy title. More often, however, associate producer can go to that person who is essentially a glorified assistant, but has been organizing the project for so damn long he or she's earned the title.

Then there is the line producer, usually called a UPM (unit production manager). This is the person on the production charged with chief oversight of the all-important budget. He must deal with everything from Tom Cruise's contract to how much the pastry chef gets paid. Epic meetings are held in the line producer's office, concerning which motel the crew will sleep in on a location shoot or should the writer be flown business class or first class.

The production accountant can usually be found darting in and out of the line producer's office, while everyone else strains to hear which of the director's production needs are being flushed away in the name of "budgetary responsibility." A line producer with a successful track record at a studio can be rewarded with a "coproducer" or even "produced by" title, but only if he's saved the studio a lot of money over the years. If they've continually run a tight ship, then the studio just bumps them up a few notches on the totem pole.

In the wonderful world of television the definitions are slightly different. The producer of a TV show is really the line producer, the one in the trenches, writing the checks, renting warehouse space, making crew deals. In TV, it's all about the executive producer. Think of Aaron Spelling or David E. Kelley or Steven

Bochco. Who wouldn't want to spend most of their time cashing residual checks from hit series?

As an assistant to someone who oversees so much, you must be prepared for a control freak. One former assistant described his boss, a hugely successful producer, as "by far the most intelligent person I've worked for, but I never thought of him as a person, he's a machine—knowledgeable, precise, a machine of intelligence." So when it comes to working for this type of boss, the margin for error is zero.

A good producer is always taking into account every conceivable option, weighing them against each other, looking to see how much the project can benefit at the smallest cost. Their minds can be far-reaching. A good producer can catch a sloppy agent who has let a deal point slip by unnoticed. This mentality can be a nightmare for an assistant. You can't get away with anything. To say most producers are detail-oriented is a massive understatement.

The actual skills necessary to assist a producer are really no different from those required by an assistant to an agent/manager or a studio exec. Specifically, heavy phones, filing, scheduling pitches, general office duties. Whereas those jobs are a constant hamster wheel of stress, life in a production company is feast or famine depending on the all-important "green light." If your boss is making a movie, things will be busy but exciting, educational, and upbeat. If not, things may be easier around the office, but the mood can become stormy and dark with the fear that nothing will get made and the studio deal will expire, taking you with it.

Nonetheless, assisting a producer is a great job for those who want to pursue agenting/managing, thanks in large part to the phenomenon known as "packaging." Packaging is basically when an agency or management company puts together the different elements to make a movie or TV project, using their roster of clients to take home a bundle, known as the "packaging fee." Producers do much the same kind of putting together of a project, but for a "producing fee."

Management companies are producing more and more these days. Agents are jumping ship left and right so that they can hop on the unregulated managerial bandwagon and take home producing fees in addition to management commissions. One of the most high-profile, recent examples of this occurred when Arnold Rifkin left his post as president of the William Morris Agency to manage clients like Whoopi Goldberg, Bruce Willis, and Danny Glover.

This job is also a good stepping stone to agenting/managing because you will get a glimpse into the world of contract negotiations. A producer has to think like a lawyer with a keen eye for the small print of every contract and deal memo. It is the producer who is responsible for the budget of the picture and has to know exactly how much everyone is making and for what. Then there are the legal clearances, the music rights, and the inevitable lawsuits when some crackpot writer accuses your boss of ripping off the great script he sent in years ago, which bears no resemblance to anything.

But this last situation brings up an important lesson for producers' assistants. Never read unsolicited material, scripts sent directly from authors, unless the author signs a release form stating he won't sue you when he sees your boss's Uma Thurman movie featuring a landlady with the same name as the landlady in his script. One assistant made this mistake when she tried to be polite to a pushy, novice screenwriter who continually called the producer's office to get feedback on her terrible script about a serial killer. The assistant allegedly said she enjoyed the script (implying she had read it) and mentioned a project that the producer was working on that also dealt with a serial killer. Well, when the writer bombed out with her lousy script, she decided to start a bogus legal action against the producer in an effort to extort money. The crux of her argument rested on her claim that since his assistant had allegedly read her serial killer script, the producer had access to her brilliant ideas. So as an assistant, watch what you say and what you read, and become very familiar with the phrase "I'm sorry, we don't accept unsolicited submissions."

This job can also help those of you who want to become writers or directors, because you get a really good look at how the whole picture comes together across the desk of a producer. As a writer, you might benefit from seeing how the "other side" thinks, which will make it easier for you in development meetings further down the road (that is, if you ever finish that script you're writing about your uniquely dysfunctional family, the one you foolishly thought you'd be able to write during your "spare time"). If you're lucky and your boss lets you poke your head into meetings from time to time, you'll have the privilege of witnessing the great Hollywood pastime: the illustrious "story meeting." This is where your boss and his development cohorts work with writers to hone pitches, original scripts, adaptations, rewrites, etc.

And of course, because so much business is done over the phone, you will certainly overhear writers being pimped by their agents, writers pitching concepts, writers receiving script notes from impossibly inarticulate, simple-minded, and aggressively excited D-girls and their semiattentive bosses who say things like, "Don't be afraid to go to those dark places." You'll hear literary agents negotiating rewrites, writers getting replaced by newer, hipper, edgier writers, and so on and so on and so on. You get to watch the development process from first to final draft and if you've got the time and the inclination, you can read the various drafts and learn either how to improve a movie from its initial inception, or, as in most cases, learn how a good idea can be destroyed by too many cooks, too many compromises, and way too much money down the development drain.

You can learn what a producer is going to want to hear from a writer and you'll learn how notes are given. You should expect to type up pages of things like:

- "We're not saying Mel Gibson can't be a killer, just make him a likable killer."

- "Take out heroin, change it to pot. Pot's funny, heroin is not."
- "We don't buy that a stewardess would have a summer estate."
- "One way to up the romantic tension would be a quick sex scene right before the Travolta character dies of cancer."
- "Instead of 'retarded' can we say '*Rain Man*-esque'?"
- "Make the black love interest Hispanic; by the time this movie's released, their 'buying power' will have doubled."
- "Make her younger. Sean Connery's love interest cannot be forty years old. The man is a stud, for Christ's sake."

Similarly, if you want to be a director, it can't hurt to learn how to use a producer's eye for the big picture. Directors and producers share the task of having to keep everyone on the set in high spirits, while simultaneously demanding as much output as can be squeezed. While in production on a picture, producers can be diplomats in constant negotiations with bordering, volatile nations (the writer, the director, the actors, the crew, and the money men). They'll start out as everyone's friend, but when push comes to shove, they will scream and yell and fire off faxes and threaten careers just to get things done the right way. Remember, these are people whose job it is to not take "no" for an answer.

Like top agents and executives, top producers often have several assistants. Usually they have one or two, but busy producers can have up to five or six assistants at a time, on one or both coasts. One deals exclusively with the phones, one with errands, one with script submissions, one deals with personal stuff, and maybe another assists them.

If you are a first, or even second, assistant to a producer, exploit the relationship. Remember, producers want to be on top of everything, so keep them in the loop about news, gossip, trends, hot young talent, etc. The one thing they always need is material: new plays, articles, books, and scripts. After all, it was someone in producer Lauren Schuler Donner's office who came up with the idea of remaking *Little Shop Around the Corner* as *You've Got Mail*.

So do research on the side for new projects or projects in development. Read every magazine. Be the "on it" person and they'll remember that you were the first person to tell them about this or that. And, finally, schmooze the contacts, because if you want to be a producer, one day they'll be your contacts, too.

GOD IS IN THE DETAILS AND, PRACTICALLY SPEAKING, SO IS YOUR JOB

Here's a sample day for a producer's assistant, ripped from her legal pad:

To Do:

• Bawl out the gardener for not being able to find the right-size pots for the banana trees.

• Schedule a drinks meeting with [a no-name director] who's attached to [a star].

• Stalk the Air Touch cellular rep to get boss the "hands-free" phone. [Day twenty of this task]

• Find out what time he wants his massage. Raphael can only come after four on Saturday, or before six on Sunday.

• Get the right pots for the banana trees.

• Schedule a meeting with [a magazine editor].

• Schedule for [a writer] to come in for a pitch.

• Check smarterliving.com for weekend vacation deals.

• Check his stocks.

• Write and send pass letters for William Morris submissions.

• Research every kind of computer that has an internal film-editing capacity. Cross-reference and call every computer dealer in Los Angeles area.

• Call the gardener again to tell him I tracked down the right pots.

• Look up all blond actresses from the fifties for a joke in the script.

- Order a chain, a black collar, biscuits, bones, and chew toys from the Fosters & Smith dog supply catalogue.
- Arrange for bulk purchasing antidepressants through Walgreens.

If you find that list daunting, then this job is definitely not for you. And this is nothing compared to what assistants to major producers have told us in researching this book. For example, one producer has the endearing habit of physically assaulting his assistants. Another demanded that explanations be given for each of the thousands of names Paramount invited to the premiere of his movie. One producer expects pens to be placed a certain way on his desk.

"I learned everything that I didn't want to do, all the ways I don't want to work," is how one former assistant summed up his time working for a maniacal producer. He was promoted to first assistant because he memorized three thousand phone numbers in six weeks. "I cried at home after work. I was so passionate about the biz, working for one of the best producers in the business. But there's nothing worse than doing a great job and trying really hard, all you want to do is succeed, and then to get abused so badly—it didn't matter what you did. You'd always get abused. Never a word of praise when you did something right, or better than right."

So what's the upside? "Working for this guy was as awful as you can imagine, he was petty and cruel and a total slob with bad breath, he hadn't been to the dentist in literally fifteen years. But to sit in the room with the best writers and directors was an incredible experience, I have no regrets." And he's not alone:

"There's an unwritten code, the boys' club code, and it's a membership that lasts the entirety of your life in the business. Everybody whose worked for one of, you know, *those* producers [the kind who has a "team" of assistants, usually on both coasts] knows it. Eighty-five percent of those former assistants all stay in touch, it's a fraternity. Even if they don't like each other, they still call each other back."

Another former colleague agrees. "It was everybody in that room against the boss. When he'd scream at someone, we'd all support each other."

The late, great producer Marvin Worth *(Lenny, The Rose, Malcolm X)* was, as one former assistant describes, " . . . crotchety, on drugs, really the most evil person in the world. . . . He was brutal, he took people's lives and reproduced them and he lived his life the same way. He was a caricature, a comic book character who did well. His attitude was either you suck or you're nothing. But he fought with blood, sweat, and tears to make a true movie. It had to be true to the story. He would do illegal things to find the truth. He would not make the movie if one line was not true. He put his life on the line."

When a perfectionist producer doesn't get his way, you'd better steer clear. If all else fails, they figure, screaming, throwing things, and kicking is always worth a shot. One producer threw a temper tantrum in the hallways of the studio where he had a deal. Said his then-assistant, "He flipped out and kicked a hole in the wall next to the elevator. It was really funny because his foot got stuck in the hole after he kicked it in, he was sort of hopping around trying to keep his balance, all the while swearing at the top of his lungs." The elevator doors opened and before stepping in, the assistant quickly attempted to cover the damage with a fake plant. The next day the producer entered the office screaming, "Why the fuck haven't you had that hole fixed?!" Talk about a lose-lose situation. "Yes, sir, I'm on it," is the only answer.

But is there a place to draw the line? Check out the following true story and see what you would have done: A New York–based producer has to go location scouting upstate on a weekend, so of course he drags along his assistant, who has to watch him eat his way up and down the Henry Hudson Parkway, slobbering over McNuggets and frozen yogurt and endless bottles of Snapple all day. The assistant foolishly thought she might enjoy a day away from the headset, a day of actual moviemaking.

Cut to: the late afternoon, the sun's going down, her boss has indigestion, and is making her track down a bus station "somewhere near Woodstock" where the director thought he remembered seeing "a certain kind of waiting area" with these great "orange connected chairs that have individual TV sets attached." After a tour of upstate bus stations, none of which featured individual TV sets, the producer and assistant head back to Manhattan. He's cursing and throwing empty Coke cans at her the whole time. "You are finding me those chairs, all right?!"

Now, the plot thickens once you realize that when you pass the bridge to the Henry Hudson Parkway, there are no rest stops again until you get into Manhattan, which can take somewhere between one and two hours, depending on the traffic.

Well, the Sunday night traffic is hideous. Soon enough her boss is whining, "I really have to go to the bathroom." The whining doesn't cease, an hour passes, the traffic crawls. No Jiffy John in sight. He pulls to the side of the road and, with one hand on his bladder, he says, "Give me that empty Snapple bottle!"

And right there, right in front of her, he unzips his pants, while mumbling, "You don't understand . . . " and relieves himself with great force into the Diet Mango Madness bottle. He immediately fills it, says, "Get me another," and she does so while trying to look away, but has to focus for long enough to take the urine-filled Snapple bottle from him. "Get rid of it." A drop hits her finger when the bottle tips a little as she clumsily tries to open the window to throw it out. She does the same with the next bottle and then has to wait another forty-five minutes before she can get to a bathroom to clean her hands. You can bet that from that day forward, she only answers, "no" to the question, "Snapple?"

Assisting a Studio Executive: An Ideal Job for Someone in the Witness Protection Program

If you want to make movies come to Hollywood; but unless you pay the price, you won't succeed! When you get off the train in Los Angeles, you're practically thrown into the street . . . and no matter which direction you choose or how much time you take to get your bearings, any one of these streets intersecting in front of you and taking off in straight lines to the east, to the west, to the south, to the north, ends fatally at a wall. The wall is the famous Great Wall of China that surrounds every studio and that makes Hollywood, already a difficult city to conquer, a true forbidden city. . . .

—Blaise Cendrars, *Hollywood: Mecca of the Movies*

In recent years, studios have tightened their belts as production slates call for fewer films. For the majors, the name of the game these days is a bigger gamble on a smaller number of releases, à la *Titanic.* They'll gladly trade you five Meryl Streep movies for one Adam Sandler vehicle. If you are fortunate enough to snag one of the fewer and fewer jobs assisting one of the ever-shrinking number of studio executives, you will find it necessary to imbibe Hollywood's version of the corporate mentality. Don't expect the usual corporate culture of standing around the water cooler discussing last night's WWF match and who's going to pay for happy hour at TGI Friday's. No, the studio corporations and their employees tend to be more sophisticated than that. And more elusive. Impossible to nail down. Think Stepford execs. And as an assistant to a Stepford exec, you will need to adopt some similar traits.

Here's a test to see if you've got what it takes for this job. If you can look in the mirror and say the following sentences, without flinching, you're a natural:

- "Robin, Christmas just wouldn't have been the same without *Patch Adams.*"
- "You know, it's really refreshing to see a movie like *Booty Call.*"
- "Welcome aboard, Calista, I'm sure you're exactly what Shakespeare had in mind when he wrote *A Midsummer Night's Dream.*"
- "That's what makes HBO different, Sinbad. We'll put you in a western."
- " . . . Cut to Sandy Bullock on a Vespa."
- "Okay, are you sitting down, Mr. Eisner . . . *Air Bud 2: Golden Receiver.*"
- "Come on, Sylvester Stallone trapped in a tunnel for two hours, it's brilliant!"
- "Geena Davis as a pirate? Now that's a film I can get behind."
- "We see this as an event movie, Brandi."

If you didn't do well on the test, not to worry. For extra credit, just pad your score, blame someone else, and pretend it never happened. After all, that's what an aspiring studio exec would do!

To be fair, serving as an executive at a studio can be quite difficult. With the exception of the one or two heads of production, most execs have to say "no" to agents, writers, and directors all day long and then when they want to say "yes" they have to go to their boss. Their primary responsibility does not differ greatly from that of producers; they solicit material that they then push or "shepherd" through the studio system. The difference is, they are continually parroting the party line—get a big star, keep costs down, make everyone "likable." It is difficult for execs to stay loyal to a studio and to a project. And if push comes to shove, very few execs will take on their studio superiors to defend a filmmaker. Fortunately, the assistants will never become part of those dialogues.

Despite their title, creative executives often must play the bad cop to the talent. They must ask the irritating yet crucial questions that can turn an idea into a movie or TV show. How much will it cost? Can they get a star? Does the director have foreign appeal? Would they change the gay best friend to a black best friend? Can they cut twenty pages from the second act of the script? Is there a part for Ricky Martin?

As soulless and boorish as that may sound, it gets worse. If you find a job opening with a studio's "production exec" you should do some homework and figure out if that means physical production (as opposed to creative). If so, then you can look forward to over-hearing questions more like, "Why do you need a four-hundred-dollar microphone?" and "Does Gérard Depardieu know that foie gras is not a craft services item?" For some, such as those assistants interested in becoming line producers, this can be an educational experience in the nuts and bolts of how production really works—dealing with Teamster unions, salaries for costume designers, prop department budgets, etc. If not, well . . . at least you'll learn how to disguise money for hookers as a transportation budget item.

On the creative side, studios generally break down into the following levels, starting at the top of the food chain:

- *Chairman of the Studio* ("Hi, I oversee a film studio, record label, TV studio, animation department, and interactive division and basically I'm set for life.")
- *President of Motion Picture Group* ("Hello, I probably won't ever become chairman, but after my huge Adam Sandler movie they had to promote me above the president of production, hence the vaguely fancy title.")

- *President of Production* ("Yes, I am the one with the ulcer down here in the trenches making the tough day-to-day decisions and deals that those beneath me are powerless to execute and those above me are all too happy to criticize. Thank God I'm paid seven figures and have an expense account the size of Angelina Jolie's lips.")

- *Executive or Senior VP of Production* ("You can call me Dan Quayle, the guy who's just waiting for his turn at bat. Polite and appropriately deferential, I would hate to see the president of production slip and fall down a flight of stairs or get on an ill-fated flight to St. Martin. That would be a shame.")

- *Several VPs of Production* ("Often referred to as the seven dwarves, you'll find one of us sleepy, one grumpy, and at least one dopey.")

- *Creative Executives* ("Call us 'CEs.' Call us 'buddy' or 'pal' if you don't remember our names when you pass us in the hall. Call us at midnight to ask us to read the book or script you were supposed to. Call us a cab when you see us wasted at weekend parties, trying to forget about the rat-trapped-in-a-maze life we lead during the week.")

- *Story Editor* ("Well, I'm not really an editor, but I do read a lot of stories and write a lot of coverage and oversee all the other readers chained down here in the basement with me. I've got some helpful comments on structure and character arc, if you'd ever return my call.")

- *Readers* ("Help!!! Help!!! They've got us trapped here in the sweatshop working day and night for only—" *thud*, followed by a scream.)

A studio exec may have graduated from an Ivy League with a master's thesis on *Beowulf*, only to find himself sitting across from Chris Tucker saying, "I read the latest draft of *Rush Hour 3*, and what can I say, I got chills." Check your honest opinions at the studio gate please. For a sophisticated mind this can be difficult but for the most part, studio executives either swallow their capacity for original thought and relax in the backyard of the house that *The Bodyguard* paid for or they simply fail to notice that they are being transformed into Team America culture vultures.

Studio executives don't walk out of movies and say, "I loved it, it was brilliantly nuanced and terrifyingly real," they walk out and say, "This is a tough one, because tonally it's just not going to play well for Joe Blow in middle America." Who is this mythical man? All of Hollywood is consumed by his needs and desires, this guy who loves *Home Improvement* and *Lethal Weapon 4*. You may hope you never meet him. But he is, in a twisted way, the most powerful man in Hollywood. He calls the shots.

As much as Joe Blow rules the studio, so does A-list talent. It's all about a star. Story or no story, who cares, Demi Moore is stripping. It's that simple. Of course, most executives flatter themselves with their "pet projects," which are often fascinating, original stories about social injustices or radical outsiders and almost always end up in "turnaround." Let's face it, we're talking about an industry that took almost a decade to bring something as "controversial" as *Shakespeare in Love* to the silver screen; there were objections to Shakespeare's implied love for a lad, even if it was Gwyneth Paltrow *dressed* as a lad.

In fairness, not all these people are monsters. It's good business to rave to Don Johnson about his performance in *Tin Cup*. Diplomacy. Cheeriness. Always, and we mean always, "excited about the project." In fact, one young writer got a call from a Miramax exec who was delivering the bad news that if some legal points in the writer's deal were not cleared up, the project was going to be abandoned. Naturally, the exec ended the call with, "We're still very excited about the project."

If you've shelled out the bucks for this book to get the skinny on Hollywood, you've undoubtedly seen Robert Altman's *The Player*. Tim Robbins plays a studio executive who is basically a shrewd coward who literally gets away with murder. Suave, cunning, and politic, Robbins really nailed the essence of most of today's successful studio executives, flashing a smug grin from beneath the bubbles of a mud bath at Two Bunch Palms. A perfect image, because with studio executives rarely outlasting their two-year contracts, it's all about keeping their heads above water.

The lucky ones are allowed a bit of integrity in their daily diet of lard. For example, the same executives who were forced to make Columbia's Spice Girls movie had the opportunity to make the terrific Larry Flynt film. As an assistant, you will go on these roller-coaster rides alongside your executive boss.

Now that you have a cheerful overview of the studio system, you can better prepare yourself for the role of assistant to one of these lucky folks. Your main responsibilities will include scheduling pitches, logging scripts and directors' reels, and dealing with the producers on the studio lot who have deals with your specific executive.

The day-to-day duties consist primarily of administrative stuff, placing calls to agents, writers, and directors, soliciting projects, and responding to the usual batch of projects in which John Travolta might star as a man half his age and weight who is strongly attracted to women. However, as an assistant in a studio, in a certain sense you will do less work than other assistants because you don't have to do the story notes, the casting lists, the coverage, or even much of the filing. It all comes from the bottom up. There are even people assigned just to do the copying.

Your life begins and ends on the studio lot. You get there by eight-thirty or nine and put in ten to twelve hours, you eat at the studio commissary, you see the same people every day, give the guard at the gate the same vacant smile every morning as you arrive and every night when you leave, and perhaps most important, you hydrate all the writers, directors, stars, and producers who meet with your boss. Hollywood is thirsty and you are its cocktail waitress. Your job is to offer anyone who comes in for a meeting something to drink: "Snapple? Sparkling water or flat?" A writer coming in for a meeting is like a man on death row and you are the warden saying, "Any last requests?"

It's eerily quiet as you sit in your glorified cubicle decorated with framed posters of movies the studio did way back when it had artistic vision, starring the likes of Clark Gable and/or Claudette Colbert, while you wonder why you're messengering Nic Cage the latest draft of *8MM*. The quiet belies the fact that on phone calls behind closed mahogany doors, millions of dollars are exchanging hands.

Let's discuss decor for a second, simply because this is your world and this is the world you must reflect. The studios all harken back to their glory days: Columbia is Nouveau Deco, Paramount is thirties bungalow chic, Disney is pomo Frank Gehry tomorrowland, Warner Bros. brings to mind *L.A. Confidential*, the wooden venetian blinds to keep the sun from distracting the executives as they discuss the latest Wesley Snipes vehicle; the seven dwarves over the entrance to the Team Disney building "pee" on you when it rains. Universal is the only lot that is out-and-out ugly, except for the newly remodeled Fox lot, which features a waterfall cascading in front of what is usually a poster for Drew Barrymore's latest atrocity, advertising the former *Playboy* centerfold as a virgin . . . again.

The studio is a fat place to work. There is fat everywhere: the lavish gifts given for any reason; the nonstop messenger service; the FedEx-ing of everything, even locally. It's the land of corporate America, excessively wasteful during the prosperous times. Since every thought turns into a memo, "cc" everyone on everything, and make twenty extra copies.

Of course, studios can afford to be wasteful thanks to their double-bookkeeping system and a phenomenon known as "soft dollars." Studios are one big tax scam. They charge themselves for everything, so no film ever makes a profit. Not even *Forrest Gump* showed a net profit. Why? Because they overcharge themselves for renting their own stages and equipment, then charge themselves interest on the amount due. Then they charge themselves for all the overhead, payroll, and administration fees they need in order to collect the bill from themselves. Then they pay interest on that. Around and around it goes, until you end up in court like Art Buchwald after *Coming to America*, fighting to prove that huge hits actually do make money and studios are not nonprofit organizations.

But there's a smug, silent satisfaction in being the buyer instead of the seller. And as a studio employee, feel free to join the club, looking down on those not working at a studio. But be respectful of your colleagues within the company. You'll find other studio assistants are mainly young kids on the climb out of college or middle-aged women from the valley, probably divorcées with no skills and untapped maternal instincts. These women land jobs to certain execs who just want a solid, robotic, drama-free secretary to deal with their lives. Sure, these gals might not work overtime, but they're not going to start bucking for a promotion either.

The bottom line with studio assistant jobs is really this: No one will notice you. Ever. Unless you're working for the one or two executives in the studio who actually have the power to green light a project, you will be virtually invisible to those on the outside and your chances for promotion within the company are slim to none.

Studios rarely promote their own, perhaps because assistants know too much about their bosses' flaws. And, unlike other companies, they have union readers so studios don't encourage assistants to read. They may promote people in the story department, but rarely assistants.

So what's the upside of studio jobs? The better pay (although nowhere near the executives' $200,000 to $3,000,000 a year), a more civil working environment, and excellent benefits. In other words, if the new Prada coat is more important to you than being recognized at Morton's, this is the job for you.

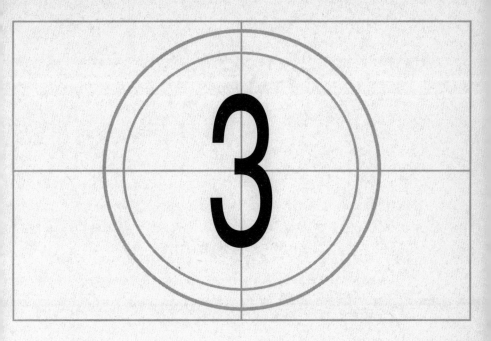

FINDING YOUR PLACE AMONG THE STARS

What to Do If Your Last Name Isn't Spielberg

I discovered early in my movie work that a movie is never any better than the stupidest man connected with it.

—Ben Hecht, *A Child of the Century*

Now that you've decided which ladder to climb, assistant job openings can be found through various channels. You'll find them in the back of *Variety, The Hollywood Reporter,* and in the job listings that are posted on interagency and studio e-mail. The UTA job list is one of the most effective resources. And look online at one of the ever-increasing Hollywood dot-coms. Another popular route is to send e-mails to every company listed in the Creative Directory. You might get lucky if you send out a blind mailing. But that's sort of like putting a token in the Megabucks slot machine thinking you'll win the $38 million jackpot.

The best proven way to get your first job is through connections and personal referrals. This is especially the case if you're looking to assist a star. Famous people rarely hire someone who doesn't come via a trustworthy connection. But even if you think you have no connections to the movie business, you probably do. One young ingenue arrived in Hollywood thinking she knew nobody, so she got a nonpaying internship at a small production company run by a bunch of screenwriter/producer hipsters. After a couple of months, she tagged along to an industry party where she met someone who had graduated from her high school six years earlier. They chatted and it turned out their fathers were coworkers and they both had a crush on the same punk rocker from their hometown. Based on these common threads, the older of the two, a working screenwriter, recommended her fellow alumnus to a thriving director/actor in need of an assistant. So much for no connections. Only three months after moving to Los Angeles she was being paid well, with benefits and perks, and loving her job.

There are many lessons to be learned from this story. First of all, never assume that you have no connections. Second, get an internship while you are looking for a job, if you can afford to. This is how you might find that long-lost connection or make new ones. And last, make the party rounds. It can be a very effective way of at least hearing about what's out there. You can accomplish the equivalent of a month's worth of phone calls just by hanging around a keg in some mail room jockey's backyard.

THE SCHMOOZE

Rule number one: Never talk about a project when you first meet people at a party. Talk about something else. They're out drinking, trying to dull the pain of selling out, and they might not want to be reminded that they have to do last-minute production notes on the movie you just brought up. Being too aggressive about the "biz" makes people think you want something from them (of course you do, but you can't show it). As a general rule, trying too hard indicates that there must be something wrong with you. Be as likable as you can be, even though you're probably terrified that you'll never get a job and your parents are on the verge of cutting you off from the minuscule allowance you're barely existing on.

Unlike most of America, where meet-and-greets involve name tags and Styrofoam cups of coffee in Marriott Renaissance conference rooms, Hollywood is all about being attractive and hanging out in the right places. Hollywood is high school, and if you want to be accepted by the older crowd and the cool kids, you want to be cute and have a great personality. This isn't to say that you'll meet your future boss at Indochine, but you may meet the guy who knows the guy who knows your future boss.

LEMME TELL YOU A STORY . . .

Learn how to tell a story. Cocktail parties for someone in your position are like talk show spots for a new actor trying to promote his first big movie. Prepare your "bit," and be ready to improvise and quip from the cuff. Hollywood is all about selling stories: if you can't do that, you're out. Rather than selling yourself by prattling on about your ambitions, tell a story, a story that has nothing to do with Hollywood or your need for a job. If you can sell someone on your ability to engage an audience, then you've made an important impression.

It's critical to know right off the bat who you can learn the most from, who will be loyal, and how to detect bullshit along the way. For example, the seemingly sonorous "suits" often have the most important contacts that can help get your résumé into the right hands. Lawyers and agents have clients who usually respect their advice and recommendations, so if you find yourself at a Hollywood party flirting with your favorite *Will and Grace* star, it may be worthwhile to excuse yourself and chat up the dour-looking dealmaker in the corner. These are the guys who do the favors and are owed the favors. Always a good place to start job hunting.

Beware the social climber who appears too interested in becoming your "pal" and has a tendency to ask too many questions. These types are self-interested and tend to step over you after using whatever information and contacts you provide. The best move you can make is finding a mentor. Someone older, with experience, who is not competitive or threatened by a newcomer. You might find such a mentor in a boss (though this can become conflicted if and when you move on to another job) or you may find someone in a social context. Many mail room trainees strike up relationships with those to whom they deliver on a daily basis, at offices throughout Hollywood.

DO'S AND DON'TS

They may seem obvious, but you'd be surprised at how often the simplest of these pointers are ignored.

DO: Smile politely at everyone's jokes, no matter how lame, but don't laugh audibly, thereby committing yourself to God knows how unpopular a Hollywood parasite.

DON'T: Tell everyone about the great theater project you did in your hometown.

DO: Nod enthusiastically when hearing praise for any movie that's crossed the hundred-million-dollar mark. (Note: When discussing any Robin Williams movie, be sure to add the caveat, "Well, people seem to just love that stuff.")

DON'T: Be seen disappearing into the bathroom with Robert Downey Jr. and/or Christian Slater.

DO: Get names and phone numbers and a commitment, no matter how drunken, that you may call that person the next day.

DON'T: Ask any writer, director, or actor what they've done. (However, when they tell you the name of their unproduced pilot for Lifetime, DO nod enthusiastically.)

DO: Go home and look up their credits online: try the IMDB (Internet Movie Database). It's easy because it's free. You can also try the Creative Directory for producers, or *VideoHound* for actors and directors.

DON'T: Be the first to arrive or the last to leave.

If you've committed any of the **DON'TS** above, please . . .

DON'T: Mention that you've read our book. We don't want to be associated with you.

OUR RECIPE FOR HUMBLE PIE

. . . is to ask the right questions in the right situations. No one wants to hear how much a twenty-two-year-old thinks he knows about the movie business. Nor is this the best way for a twenty-two-year-old to take advantage of a meeting with someone more experienced. Be clear about your ambitions, but never pretend to know more than you do. People in this business love to dole out advice; take advantage of this.

Similarly, you should be aware of the necessity of research, homework, and the follow-up. Before meeting someone, always figure out what they do, what they've done, and what their reputation is. Keep track of each encounter and follow up. If someone recommends a book, read the book and then send a thank-you note. If he or she offers to put you in touch with a colleague, be sure to follow up and contact that person. If, in the cold light of day, your contact does not seem to remember the offer, just be persistent. Keep calling. Eventually, they'll figure out it's easier to help you than to say no to you.

DROPPING NAMES . . . AND CATCHING THEM

In conversations and interviews, people may gossip and it may be tempting to offer up an opinion or a tidbit. But, given your neophyte position, silence is the golden rule. That is not to say, however, that you cannot benefit by taking in what you hear. Most often, all gossip is true, if for no other reason than because everyone believes it to be true. But to those looking to hire an assistant, the most important traits are those of trustworthiness and discretion. Don't be a chatterbox.

Similarly, you may find it tempting to drop a name or two. Like someone of status whom you've recently met or your father's business partner's celebrity son. In these cases, name-dropping (as opposed to gossip) may actually be helpful in establishing your position in the world. It can give employers some perspective on where you think you belong. However, a little bit goes a long way. And even though it is common Hollywood practice to drop names of people to whom you've said only two words, be careful not to overstate the extent of your "in"-ness. At this point in your career it is perhaps less important to drop names than to catch them. This is how you learn the business, the players, and it will give you a point of reference for your interviews.

In addition, if you have a special knowledge of something (Buddhism, rock climbing, modern architecture . . .) try to seamlessly convey this in conversation. Show that you take an interest in life. Nothing is more tiresome than an unemployed newcomer ignorantly reiterating yesterday's industry news to someone trying to relax and have a drink after work.

WHAT TO DRINK AND WHERE TO ORDER IT

The entire movie business is built on a collective desire for anything new or what is often referred to as "hip and edgy." If you can tip someone off to a funky, Creole breakfast joint or a dive karaoke bar downtown, you get points. As an assistant, you will inevitably have to plan a party (Hollywood's equivalent of White House cabinet meetings), and your boss will want to thrill guests with a venue that is about to be hip.

We'd love to give you an "in and out" list, but things change so rapidly it's impossible. There are bars in L.A., The Smog Cutter for example, that were derelict fleabags just a few years ago (Bukowski was a regular at this one) and are now crammed with nightmare Hollywood types "keeping it real" on the east side. The Hollywood Hills Diner was once empty but for the few out-of-towners staying in the Best Western upstairs, but since it was revamped and featured in the cult hit *Swingers*, it's impossible to eat there without overhearing the latest teen movie sensation ordering scrambled egg whites or a screenwriter describing the arc of his "Courteney Cox character."

BE ALL THAT YOU CAN BE

During the weeks before you begin your first Hollywood assistant job, you may feel like an idiot hiking on a treadmill with a book like this catching your sweat, but this is all part of the pre–Tinsel Town, postcollege mental and physical training you must endure.

For most humans, the likelihood of maintaining a regular exercise ritual after the first month as an assistant is next to nil. So try to get into shape before you start your job, so that at least you've got some muscle to help dispense with the "empty calories" of office junk food and the studio commissary french fries that you will absolutely need to get you through to your 8 P.M. office departure time. A daily cardio workout of half an hour at least gets the blood to the brain, makes you more efficient, and better able to absorb new material, like six hundred phone numbers within the first two weeks of your new job. And the endorphins will help quell the murderous rage you will surely feel toward your boss during the early days on the job.

Get to bed early, but only after your required three hours of nightly television watching. This does not include the video rental crash film class you'll be undertaking on the weekends. Make sure to catch at least one of the trashy behind-the-scenes

Hollywood gossip shows. *Entertainment Tonight* is an obvious classic with its shameless promotion of studio blockbusters. *Access Hollywood* tends to spin a more dramatic tale, suspect though it often is, and while the E! Network can be highly informative and extremely enlightening, you'll find that you have to dodge endless makeovers and relatively useless gossip about Hollywood outsiders, such as Donald Trump and Kate Moss, to get to the good stuff.

Once you're through with that, move on to a steady surf among all the unexciting sitcoms that have been concocted by humorless, "demographic-pleasing" network programmers. Just make sure you know the names of the stars and practice making speeches about how TV just isn't what it was back in the Mary Tyler Moore/*M*A*S*H* days, and how you want to help change that.

You can also form little sound bites in your head summarizing each network's profile: "USA, once based purely in the commerce of tits and ass, is now taking programming risks by hiring young, independent feature start-ups like the Pate Brothers." Or, "CBS: it's not just for seniors anymore."

Next you're on to the teen, hospital, or police procedure one-hour drama of your choice. This is where the execs go shopping for the next Claire Danes or George Clooney. Now it's time for bed. You don't have to watch Leno and Letterman, just be aware of who's pushing what (easily ascertained from *TV Guide*).

Of course, you have to keep abreast of the cable event movies and have at least a sense of what the latest, scandalous news stories are. People in Hollywood are always impressed by someone who actually knows the name of whichever baby was kidnapped or dropped down a well in the heartland this week.

Watch as many movies as you can. This should be fun, but you should take it seriously. You should have a passion for knowing details about film history. You should think like that geek at the video store who delivers a thesis on each video as he scans and bags it. Details! Get whatever comprehensive film guide you can find and look things up while watching each movie. It's more about memorizing information than about college film classes. In other words, less like, "The desire to desire: female subjectivity in the films of Alfred Hitchcock." More like, "Stockard Channing's still working . . . good for her."

The New York assistant has the added advantage of working in close proximity to both great theater and major book publishers. These two venues provide fertile ground for movie and television ideas. Who knows? Getting your hands on an early book manuscript or the rights to an off-off-Broadway play could shortcut your trip to the top.

Padding Your Résumé: It's No Less Ethical Than the Wonderbra

"For twenty years, I washed his shorts, I ironed them, and I starched them!"
"You did all that?"
"Yeah, well, I supervised."
    —*The First Wives Club*

After you've made contacts with people willing to accept your résumé, this all-important document will be representing you in offices throughout Hollywood. So pad it. This is not to say you should outright lie. That's never a good idea, no matter what the circumstance. However, you can reasonably argue that checking your e-mail a lot makes you "an experienced systems analyst." And who is going to know that "1995" refers only to the summer? Give people what they want. For example, an actress with a baby may care that you studied child development in school. A single agent in his twenties will probably not. Craft your résumé for the particular job, even if it means revising it for every interview. The best advice is to research the prospective boss and have a strong handle on what he has done, is doing, and needs.

To cite an example from a related field, actor Edward Norton (unknown at the time of his audition for *Primal Fear*) did not tell the director and casting director that he was a history major at Yale with formal acting training. Instead, he "padded his résumé" by representing himself as a poor, trailer-trash Kentucky boy with a stutter. Why? Because that's what the role called for. So, take a page from Ed's book . . . he hasn't done so badly for himself.

Perhaps a better example, with a less fortunate outcome, is about a struggling, exceptionally young-looking actress/writer, who, although in her mid-thirties, re-created herself by claiming she was a teenager so that she could get a coveted staff writing position on the hit WB series *Felicity*, a job the producers wanted to fill with an "authentic teenage voice." She started as a writer and eventually even got an acting role on the show. A year into the job, someone came across her high school yearbook and blew her cover. She was fired, received the requisite bashing in *Vanity Fair* and on *60 Minutes*, and now she can't get arrested (although she could get indicted).

After you've crafted a résumé, it's time to write a cover letter. Sounds simple, right? Well, what should be a simple letter of introduction can, in the wrong hands, turn into a huge warning sign to your potential boss that reads, "I'll make you look like a complete idiot if you hire me."

To help you out, we are going to use an actual example of how *not* to write a cover letter. Here's what one hiring producer received via e-mail:

VIA E-MAIL
Attn: Human Resources
Dear Sirs or Madam:

Please accept the attach résumé for consideration for any positions in your development department, or any of your other departments that may have an opening. I would like to

mention that the production company I most recently
worked for is now in-between development deals therefore I
am available to start immediately.

As you can see from my résumé, I have a lot of experience
in many areas of television and film. I am committed to my
work, and I have the right attitude to get things done
effectively and with a smile.

Hopefully my qualifications and attitude match what you
are looking for, and we can set up a meeting to discuss my
possible future with you, and your company.

I would like to apologize for the crudeness of my résumé
via e-mail, but it is the most efficient, and least costly way of
reaching a greater number of potential employers than
traditional means. I will be glad to forward a faxed or mailed
copy of my résumé at your request.

Thank you very much for your time, and I hope to hear
from you soon.

Warm regards,
XXX
enclosure: résumé

Here's how this reads to a prospective employer:

VIA E-MAIL (**Not always such a wise idea. Though
environmentally conscious and efficient, with a click of a
button you're dismissed. Also, if an assistant prints it from
e-mail it looks bad and there's no signature. Less effort
involved than sending a real letter**.)

Attn: Human Resources (**Shows that you don't know
who you're sending it to. You're not customizing it.**)

Dear Sirs or Madam: (**Awful, specify who are you writing
to. Not to mention "sirs" is plural and "madam" is not.**)

Please accepted the attach (**Spelling mistake, sentence one, couldn't be worse, half your job is writing letters, game over!**) résumé for consideration for any positions in your development department, or any of your other departments that may have an opening. (**1. No knowledge of who you're writing to; 2. You did no homework to figure this out; 3. No specific goals; 4. Desperate.**) I would like to mention that the production company I most recently worked for is now in-between development deals (**You are telling us you are part of a failed venture. Who wants to hear the words "in between development deals"? Never associate yourself with this predicament. It's the kiss of death.**) therefore I am available to start immediately. (**Oh really, as opposed to what? We might have to get in line with all the others desperate for you to send out misspelled letters on their behalf?**)

As you can see from my résumé, I have a lot of experience in many areas of television and film. I am committed to my work, and I have the right attitude (**We'll be the judge of what's the right attitude, thanks.**) to get things done effectively and with a smile. (**This is not Starbucks.**)

Hopefully my qualifications and attitude match what you are looking for (**this is like meeting someone online who says, "Trust me, I'm good looking."**), and we can set up a meeting to discuss my possible future with you (**inappropriately sweeping and optimistic**), and your company.

I would like to apologize for the crudeness of my résumé via e-mail, but it is the most efficient, and least costly way of reaching a greater number of potential employers than traditional means. (**Don't waste time with your explanation of how you poorly chose to market yourself. All it says is you're too cheap to put a stamp on a letter, and it says we're just one on a long, anonymous list. This letter might as well start "Dear Homeowner." Awful though it is, you've made your mistake worse by apologizing for it.**) I will be glad to forward a faxed or mailed copy of my résumé at your request. (**So now we have to do the work?**)

Thank you very much for your time, and I hope to hear from you soon. (**Not likely.**)

Warm regards,

So Not Hired

enclosure: résumé

THE CASTING COUCH OF THE NEW MILLENNIUM

A typical Hollywood interview always begins with you waiting. First you wait in the reception area sipping on the Diet Mango Madness Snapple that the beleaguered assistant you are hoping to replace just handed you. Then you are ushered into your potential employer's office where you will most likely be greeted with his back to you. Instead of "nice to meet you," you'll more likely hear the final hostile words of his phone conversation in progress: "I'm not paying you to be nice to the writer, just get him to make the changes!" After slamming the headset down, he'll ask his current assistant to do about twelve things while he's interviewing. Then he will finally turn to you with a big warm smile and say, "I'm so sorry, things are crazy." Then he'll talk about himself. A lot. And you will notice how much this excites him. He'll ask you some questions that might sound like veiled threats: "You know what this job involves, right?" In other words, "We don't have to get into the details, just so long as I know, that you know, that this job is hell." And of course, you'll nod enthusiastically. He may ask you what your favorite films are, he may ask you what you want to do eventually, but often Hollywood bosses just want to know that you have just enough personality to fight for things on their behalf (dinner reservations, a discounted airfare), but not enough to demand respect in the workplace.

Having said that, you can never really predict what might go down in an interview in this town of extremes. For example, when

Bill went in for his interview for a job as an assistant to talent
agent Susan Smith, he watched her talk on the phone for twenty
minutes, negotiating a deal for client Kathy Bates. She finally
hung up, and the conversation went like this:

"Are you Jewish?"

"No."

"You look Jewish."

"Well, I'm not."

"If you work for me, can I tell people that you *are* Jewish?"

"Sure."

"You're hired."

There are exceptional situations, so as well as advising you to
feel comfortable lying about your religion, we've got some general
words of advice for the crucial first impression. Let's start with
the most important thing first: appearance. No cologne, no per-
fume. You're not applying for a job as the CK spritzer boy. Here's
a cautionary tale: A highly recommended, experienced assistant
had been waiting years for one of the coveted positions as assistant to a top agent. The agent looked at his résumé and experience and practically hired him on the spot. However, when he
came in reeking of musk, the agent thought again. He never got
hired and heard through the grapevine some months later that it
was the Polo that did him in.

And for women, just a little makeup will do, this is not a
beauty pageant. Yes, this is Hollywood, a place where women
spend a lot of time and money on their looks. But despite the
messages contained within the pages of hair-and-makeup rags
like *In Style*, the movie business chicks tend to play down the
glamour element and refrain from excessive chatter about day
spas and slingbacks. As a professional, it's important to distin-
guish yourself from the wannabe starlet posse of out-of-work
MAWs (Model-Actress-Whatevers) i.s.o. positions as trophy
wives.

Don't walk in like Melanie Griffith in *Working Girl*. You have
to look chic and understated. If you have open-toe shoes, have a

pedicure done. Details are important. But this is not the time for your new Anna Sui Pocahontas-inspired poncho or to show off your latest piercing. Your presence in the office must compliment the decor. Your boss will want you to blend in to the point of near invisibility, but at the same time reflect the company's impeccable, classic taste. Basically, it's a Banana Republic situation. And for men, it's a variation on the classic L.A. Armani-suit-without-the-tie look.

If you want to work for a star or director, another set of rules may apply. Because these are the people always wanting to make a splash or a grand creative statement, they may be looking for a hip sidekick to tote around like the latest accessory from Fred Segal. Strident individuality in appearance can be a huge plus. Once again, study your potential employer beforehand.

The second most important thing: what to say. Basically you want to tell funny, modest stories to get the point across that you are good on your feet and you can handle anything. You want to assure your boss that you can cover her ass, yet not steal her thunder. It's a fine line. People love to talk in interviews. But it's to your advantage to listen as much as you talk. They want to know that you're someone who can listen and take directions. There are many ways to say things like, "I prioritize" and "I'm detail-oriented" without sounding like a robot. There is a balance that must be struck between having a "cheery disposition" and not having a "personality." Don't trash people in interviews. Although this is a favorite Hollywood pastime and your interviewer may even get into some backstabbing himself, resist. They want to know that you are trustworthy and will not repeat all the awful things they are going to do to you.

When it comes to salary, try not to sound desperate. Ideally, an employer wants to feel that you have a solid enough financial background so that they will not feel guilty paying you slave wages. Or feel that you might steal from them. Since most Hollywood bosses are making much more than they should be, they want to find assistants who will not resent the gross disparity too much. Downplaying salary is to your advantage in the first interview. You can haggle later. This is not to say that one must be a trust-fund brat to come to work in Hollywood. Au contraire. But if you're from humble origins, just don't make an issue of it. No Hollywood boss wants to feel guilty.

Regarding references: Always put down the highest-ranking individual you've had any kind of contact with at previous jobs or in life. You shoveled Bill Gates's snow when you were nine? Put him down. No one's going to bother him for a recommendation. And if they do, he'll probably remember you as a helpful, young neighbor. And if they bust you, they'll probably admire your spunk and hire you anyway. But be sure to warn the references that you do actually know that they may get a call and ask them to mention details that might impress the caller. Prepare and cover all your bases. What the boss says in the interview will most often be the truth about what his concerns are and what he's looking for in an assistant. So if you want the job, take the info to heart and respond accordingly.

A final obvious note: be early. It'll probably be 90 degrees on the studio lot and it'll take forever to park and find your way to their office (assume that you'll get lost and the studio gate guards will misdirect you), so just factor in the ten extra minutes it will take you to stop sweating.

Postmortem: The follow-up part of the job-seeking process can be almost as important as the interview itself. No calling every day, it's a nuisance for a busy exec. And no cutesy cards, no fruit baskets. Just an ecru note card with a few simple, intelligent sentences concerning your enthusiasm for the job. Emotions should never come into play, no matter how desperate you are. No one really cares about your hopes and dreams as much as they care about your ability to write down a phone number legibly. Send the note promptly, keep interviewing, and let fate do the rest.

Internships: How to Gain Valuable Experience While Xeroxing

I started at the top and worked down.
—Orson Welles

The obvious difference between an internship and an assistant job is that interns do not get paid. Because of this, it is far easier to get an internship. Many colleges even help place interns and give them college credit for a semester in Hollywood. So if you can afford it, and the school helps with accommodations, this is a great way to decide if you want to work your way up in Hollywood or if you want to turn around and go to film school or even drop out of the moviemaking race altogether.

No matter whom you work for, whether in development or actual production, the kinds of tasks you are given as an intern are pretty stupid. Often the people you work for do not really take you seriously, so they end up creating silly and time-consuming jobs for you just to keep you busy.

Interns are like primordial beasts staggering from the great cultivating lakes of college onto land, where they grow the legs for becoming an assistant. They are at the bottom, but they have an easier life. Not being on payroll makes it safer. Interns tend not to lose sleep worrying, like assistants do. The downside is that interns are barred from important meetings, kept on the outside, invisible, and only occasionally are they thrown a bone of advice from a superior.

THE COKEWOODS:
LIFESTYLES OF HOLLYWOOD INTERNS

When most people reflect on their internships, they will tell you, "It was fun, I partied, I got college credit. I spent most of the time boozing it up with other college students at cheap bars near the studio, having a blast and talking about how ludicrous the business is." So do it. Come and live it up at "The Oakwoods."

The Oakwoods is basically a hideous spread of apartments, not unlike a retirement village, in Burbank near the studios. Conveniently located within inhaling distance from the 101 Freeway, The Oakwoods boasts fake stucco walls surrounding acres of synthetic wall-to-wall carpeted units that you may recognize from various eighties porn. There are no windows, just one screen door, shaded by vertical blinds, which faces the other apartments. One can spy on all the child actors who come and stay there during pilot season in hopes of becoming the next Olsen or Lipnicki.

Each year college students come to The Oakwoods while working to gain credit as interns. One former resident calls it "The Cokewoods," because the kids would hang out and do drugs all night, dorm-room style, and then slap it on and show up for a clock-watching day on one studio lot or another, retabbing files in color codes or retyping various office notices like PLEASE DO NOT EAT OTHER PEOPLE'S FOOD for the refrigerator door.

For the most part though, the world of interns will consist of bong-hitting seniors, free from campus, vaguely interested in impressing their bosses who never notice them. These internships can really pay off though, despite the mundanity. An intern gets to know the office really well and takes orders from the assistant, so in a pinch, if an assistant is sick, the intern has the chance to step in and prove himself. Depending on the company (and your boss's sense of your competence) you may get to read scripts and write coverage if you work in development or you may get to tag along on a location scout if you work in production. So choose the right internship carefully to get the most out of the heady, partying days of volunteer work, so that you can trade up and get a real job once the internship expires and you are out of college. As with all jobs, the more you make them need you, the more likely you are to be brought on board as an employee.

TO DEVELOP OR NOT TO DEVELOP: PICKING THE BEST INTERNSHIP

If you work as an intern in development you learn heaps about xeroxing, answering phones (although one producer fired an intern because the tone of her voice was too high-pitched), and you run small errands. But the life-and-death importance placed on every detail in Hollywood production offices makes even an assistant afraid of letting some college kid oversee anything at all.

The upside of a development internship is that you get to read as many scripts as you can stand to read. And if they think you're smart enough, they'll let you write "coverage." Coverage is basically like writing a really bad, Cliffs Notes–inspired high school paper. Most interns start out slaving over the wording of their coverage, especially because the first time is usually a test of your abilities, but the truth is, coverage should be written simply. In fact, fancy language should be completely eliminated in favor of conveying a point. The commentary should not have the kind of analytical bias they teach you to apply in college essays, so in many ways learning to write coverage is about unlearning some of the sophistication of the college writer.

In the end, interns often become like their bosses and learn to read just the beginning and end of a script. But if you do want to get into development or producing or writing, this is a great time for you to study script structure. It is not unheard of for interns to end up spending the whole day reading.

ON THE OTHER SIDE OF THE YELLOW TAPE: INTERNING ON THE SET

If you work in production (on the set of a film or in postproduction), chances are you will work far longer hours, up to fifteen to twenty hours a day, and the job will be more labor intensive; lots of running around, holding things up, hauling props, and running to get cookies for an editor working well into the night. But you will get a bigger view than from within the four walls of a remote development office in Burbank. You will get the answers to pressing questions like, "What does a best boy do?"

Despite the drudgery of toting film mags, directing traffic, fetching coffee, and your other very important tasks, you'll get to see what goes on behind the caution line (the yellow tape that surrounds the set). Every day will have something new to offer, whether it is a new stunt, a new special effect, or some bizarre drama. It could be a crisis for the director of photography, who realizes that the proportions of the stuntwoman do not match those of the lead actress for a nude scene, it could be an actor locked in his trailer doing drugs. And all of this with everyone losing their cool and throwing fits over small, but what they consider crucial issues. It's an unwritten set policy that people are allowed to yell and go nuts and that the next day everyone forgets about it. Of course, grudges develop and fights mount and there are major, irreparable fallings-out, but you learn that everyone has to have a thick skin to get through the daily war zone intact.

Working around major movie stars may make you starstruck, but do your best to remain professional. When you find yourself standing next to the celebrities, keep quiet and try to remain in the background. You will learn that it's a big no-no to try to hitch a ride in a car occupied by a star or a producer. Trite as it sounds, you will learn that celebrities are people, too, and life's not always perfect. If you are working on a movie with Cuba Gooding Jr., for example, you will get a glimpse of what it is like to go around hearing "Show me the money" all day long.

You may also try to seek out a job in postproduction. These jobs tend to be offered mostly to kids with some technical experience. In other words, if you do know how to edit, and you have made a short film or video, or had previous internships, you might get into a postproduction house. This is a great place to start, because you spend all day with an editor or a sound mixer and you can learn a lot, just by watching. People pay a lot of money to learn how to use an AVID and people spend even more money renting or buying the equipment. But when you are an intern in post, you may learn the technical skills for free, and if you cultivate strong relationships, you might gain access to equipment for your own use. One intern at a postproduction facility in New York spent all day in the AVID room with two editors, then at night he would work on his own films and eventually he began making $80 an hour teaching people how to use the AVID during weekends. All this because the editor he worked for was so deeply grateful for the months of nonsalaried work this kid had put in when he really needed help putting his new, struggling company on the map.

BIG FISH ON A CLOSED SET

The smaller the company, the more interns will be used. While they may still depend on you for simple, boring jobs, they will grow to love you if you make it happen. You may be called upon in a crisis to do more than copy scripts. Even if you are just copying scripts because the company needs to save money on printing bills, they are going to be grateful and count you as a part of the team. Whereas fat companies with lots of employees and studio dollars to throw around will see you as an extraneous body, a nuisance whose presence may even annoy the top dog, who keeps wondering why there are all these kids knocking about the office, overhearing his private and often suspect rampages and schemes.

THE CATTLE CALL:
MAKING IT IN THE INTERN MARKETPLACE

If your college does not already have an internship program that helps guide you to a job, use the Internet. Go to your favorite search engine on the Web and type in some combination of the words "hollywood, jobs, internships," and hundreds of sites will come up. If you know that you want an internship at a particular company, call them, send them your résumé, but chances are a company will not hire a random intern, they will want to know that this person comes from a school program. Internship positions are also listed in *Variety* and *The Hollywood Reporter*.

If you are in college, however, you will learn of the Internship Fair, which can be a great place to sell yourself and to tour the possible opportunities. These occur annually. One D-girl described it as "a total meat market for hot little college boys and girls, where the sleaziest representative of the company sets up a desk, takes résumés, and circles the ones belonging to the hotties." This proves to be true, and often you'll see a lot of eye candy fiddling with coffee filters in production offices around Hollywood. But if you're not a siren with a rack or surfer with Richard Gere eyes, fear not. There are some respectable people who want the geek they know will get the job done. In fact, the most successful interns are the perky nerds, who take pencil placement and message writing seriously. Any good office manager or assistant will go for the kind of kid who looks like he's not out partying like most college kids. Also, for these types, the less glamorous and dominating the physical presence, the better.

One director of development, a gold chain–wearing guy who had already worked through a couple of last season's interns, went to the Internship Fair and hired a geeky boy, who would not threaten him, and a bombshell whom we'll call Amber. Amber was an idiot-model-whatever who wore outrageously sexy *Melrose Place* outfits and roamed around the office, casually not getting work done, and continually asking questions only pertaining to trashy gossip. The Development Dude would procrastinate from work to entertain her inquiries, but the rest of the staff couldn't stand the spectacle. One day the president of the company, who was rarely in the office, came in and was asked by the midriff-exposed Amber, "Oh my God, you had lunch with [famous actress]? I hear she is such a bitch." He closed the door on her and said to his assistant, "I can't take it, she knows about my lunch, what else? And what's with the outfits? Fire her," to which his assistant responded, "I can't fire her, she works for free, and she's halfway through her college credit." The producer barked, "No one is graduating from college by looking through our files and spreading rumors, fire her!" So the assistant had to call Amber and explain that she would get no recommendation, that her "work" had been in vain, and that she might want to consider keeping her mouth shut until she had the clout to fire off backstabbing remarks.

Meanwhile the geeky assistant was treated like royalty for his efforts, he got a gushing reference, help getting a new job, and a $600 television when he graduated from college. He later took over Development Dude's job.

MAKING IT TO THE BOTTOM: FROM VOLUNTEER TO INDENTURED SERVITUDE

Obviously, you take an internship to get your foot in the door and hope to rise to the lowest rung on the ladder: that of an assistant.

And this is pretty common. One intern at a very busy, very high-profile production company found himself in a terrifying but ultimately career-advancing spot when the head honcho producer lost both her office assistant and her production assistant in the same week. The producer was on set, battling away with the diva star of the picture and the conservative studio execs who were intent on clipping the risky but crucial elements from every scene, and suddenly her office assistant, stationed in L.A. and strapped to the phone, fell gravely ill and had to leave the job. Meanwhile, her set assistant kept screwing up to the point of getting fired. The producer was left cold and had to yank the office intern, who was still in college, to the assistant desk, to fill in for the time it would take to find a real replacement. Well, this young kid didn't even know how to roll calls (see page 129 for more on this topic), he didn't even know what the phrase meant, and the others in the office hardly had the time for daily tutorials. Suffice it to say the producer was the kind of person who could not wait around for some schmuck to figure out how to put together a conference call, so it was a sink-or-swim situation.

Lucky for the college kid, he had networked and made friends with assistants in other companies and had also memorized the rules of the office, how to call a messenger, how to handle script xeroxing, and the kind of food the boss needed delivered daily to the set. He had forged what proved to be valuable relationships with all the little people and so he was quick to learn. Not only did he become a great assistant within about a week, but he managed to parlay the freak accident into a paying job. He was pretty psyched to be taking home $600 a week, getting college credit, and knowing that after graduation he was already in place to move up.

Congratulations on Your New Job

Movie stars get millions of dollars for nothing, so when someone asks them to do something for nothing, they go crazy—they think that if they're going to talk to somebody at the grocery store, they should get fifty dollars an hour.

— Andy Warhol

$KER-CHING, KER-CHING?

Once you've landed your new job, salary negations begin . . . and end, with no regard for your financial needs. It's the law of supply and demand. You'll be lucky to get what they quoted you in the interview and that can often be as low as $300 per week, no benefits. If you start in an agency mail room it can be even less.

On the upside, there are rare occasions where an assistant can make as much as $80,000 annually, and in some cases raises and bonuses can be expected.

ASSISTANT SALARIES

Agent/Manager: Starting salary around $20,000 per year (benefits: maybe, maybe not).

Producer: Typically the starting salary is between $25,000 and $40,000, depending on whether the producer has a studio deal. There's about a 50 percent chance that you will get benefits (once again, this depends on the producer's deal). If you work for a major player you may also benefit from per diems and production top-ups to your standard salary.

A-list Director or Star: Upward of $40,000.

Studio Executive: Expect to start upward of $40,000 with benefits.

These are the standard salaries; however, there are some exceptions. Professional assistants who have no aspirations beyond the offices of the top-level entertainment moguls can take home upward of $100,000 annually, once perks, benefits, and bonuses are added in.

If you work for a real power player you can make big bucks. The good thing about working for a crazed, megalomaniacal executive or producer who manages to keep half a dozen projects afloat at any given time is that you will most likely have the opportunity to travel first class alongside your boss to all kinds of exotic (or at least Canadian) locations.

One assistant lived in a top Manhattan hotel for over a year while working as the first assistant to a producer who had to shack up presidential suite style for the shooting of his film. Many would drool at the thought of having a rent-free year at an exclusive hotel, room service, fluffy white towels, someone to turn down your bed. You can just lay back like a three-year-old and let the hotel mother you. In addition to that, his base salary of $1,000 was topped by an additional $650 per week. "I saved forty thousand dollars that year and bought my own car," recalls this assistant, "but I had no minute of being separated from the job, no retreat, nothing of my own around me, I could be reached at any hour, I hardly left the confines of that hotel, I started going completely insane." Is it worth turning into Jack Nicholson's character from *The Shining* for a bonus of $40,000? You be the judge.

Starting out is usually not quite so dramatic and even assistants with a few years' experience behind them cannot expect more than $1,000 a week.

REMEMBER, WHAT THEY DON'T PAY FOR CAN'T HURT THEM

As for benefits, good luck. They are almost never offered unless you work at a studio. However, if you do research for your boss on group health plans that may very well save the higher-ups money, and would probably cover you as well, you might luck out. Also, always look out for loopholes in the deal your employer may have with the studio, network, company, etc., that may allow for project-by-project benefits.

Quietly organize the other assistants and get your boss to agree to a group health plan so you pay only a small amount. Maybe you can convince him he's losing more on employee sick days by not covering them. And remember, for movies shooting on location, assistants are usually provided plane tickets, accommodation, and per diem. Even if it's Pittsburgh, be the first to volunteer to go on location, because if you can help out the boss, next time it could be Maui.

Other areas for negotiation include hours, vacation, and expenses. You might save thousands by getting assurance up front that your cell phone bills, parking, gas, and work-related meals can be expensed. If you are in a production job, look into overtime as well, because there has never, in the history of the job, been an assistant who did not work overtime. You might as well see if you can be paid for those long, lonely nights at the office.

The basic starting situation at most companies goes something like this:

- Hours: 9 to 8 Monday–Friday (script reading in addition to this)
- Salary: $400 to $600 per week
- Benefits: None
- Vacation: Two weeks, max., and it works around your boss's schedule.

So, keep a low overhead, hit the Barneys annual warehouse sale (you have to look good, even on this pittance of a salary), live off

the Snackwells in your office, lease a two-door Japanese car, call
your faraway relatives on your boss's dime, down the echinacea,
and try not to get sick.

Anyone who has worked in a corporate environment can tell
you there are countless ways to benefit from bureaucratic waste.
Hollywood's rich, don't feel guilty. It's a Robin Hood strategy:
take from Mickey Mouse and give to yourself.

You need to be up-to-date, right? Always on the lookout for
"material"? So order all your magazine subscriptions on the office
account. And *The New York Times* on Sunday, of course. The
office equipment is being replaced, you need a new reading lamp?
It's yours. Just don't make a greedy scene of it. Forget video rental
late fees if you're working at a major studio. Just have the studio's
in-house "video people" dupe and deliver your weekend entertainment. Why not transfer all your home movies while you're at
it? AOL subscription? Definitely a company expense. You need a
better chair because your back is killing you? Meet the Office
Depot catalogue. Ordering supplies for the office? Why not
throw in a coffeemaker? From slipcovers to picture framing,
there's always a way to hover above the poverty line with office
perks.

SHOW ME THE MONEY

After one good year it's absolutely appropriate to expect a 10 percent raise. You might be able to squeeze a little more out of your
boss after six months. It helps to negotiate this up front. It's all
about timing. The same principle used to weasel allowance out of
your parents applies. Get them in a good mood, present them
with a recent accomplishment of yours, and make the request reasonable.

Plan your strike. By the time you are in a position to ask for a
raise you should be able to anticipate your boss's mood swings the
way a meteorologist predicts hurricanes. Don't just drop the ques-

tion casually, make an appointment to review your performance. This translates pretty directly as "I want more money" so schedule the meeting for the immediate future, that way your boss doesn't have much time to think about reasons why he cannot pay you more.

Go in prepared to talk about the good work you've done, what you've learned and mastered, and have some examples of the times when you've gone above and beyond the call of duty. This is not to say that you should aggressively lobby your boss with the tedium of your extracurricular task-mastering and the hour count on your overtime. Guilt tripping only works from the powerful to the powerless, so do not attempt to make your boss feel bad. If a raise is the result of a guilt trip, you will eventually suffer at the hand of resentment. Your boss must feel that this is what is done. It's the well-if-everyone-else-is-doing-it principle that motivates most Hollywood decision making. Get your boss to feel that this is the general rule of the business, not an outlandish favor.

Of course, you'll be thinking like your boss, so have answers ready for some of the points he might attempt to make in favor of holding back a potential raise. Don't argue. Never argue. But you are allowed to begin a sentence "In fairness . . ." or "True, but you might have noticed that since that near fatal incident, I made sure that *The Hollywood Reporter* is always on top of *Variety* and to the left of your phone."

Be prepared with a specific dollar amount and the degree to which you will negotiate. Do not give an ultimatum. Unless you really want to risk the odds of getting fired, forget it. You've probably heard a lot of high-powered negotiating in the months gone by; now is not the time to mimic it. This is not a "pay-or-play" situation. You are an assistant who needs a new suit and the only "exciting, new material" you have coming in is your phone bill.

Finally, walk away with something. If they refuse to offer cash, go for the prizes: better parking, better hours, vacation time, benefits, a computer (you need the newest iMac, let's face it), a cell phone, greater responsibility in the office, an expense account, some interns on whom you can slough off responsibilities. Anything you can get your hands on. Use of the Malibu house. Be creative. And then get an idea of what it'll take for you to get a legitimate raise and when you might expect it. Try to get a commitment and a timeline out of your employer.

Keep in mind that most successful Hollywood types really have no idea about what things or people are worth. They are distanced from any real knowledge of foreign concepts like "rent" and "living expenses." They have business managers who receive their paychecks and investment dividends directly and the business managers pay the bills. Chances are, most major players do not even read their annual tax returns before signing them. So how do they know you can't live on $375 per week?

Hollywood assistants, however, get a very good idea of what the value of money can be. Most assistants share the unforgettable experience of the first visit to a boss's house. This is never a social occasion, usually it is some sort of last-minute crisis: the limo didn't show, the messenger didn't deliver the script, or the hooker overdosed. The house is generally an excessive, sprawling affair in Santa Monica, Brentwood, Bel Air, Beverly Hills, or Malibu. Chances are it is architecturally significant, though tastelessly overfurnished by one of the three popular interior designers who have cornered the market on overstuffed couches and Eames chairs.

Some lucky assistants enjoy the perks of house-sitting or even vacationing with their employers. Meg Ryan's assistant, for example, spent quality time in Montana on Meg and husband Dennis Quaid's stunning ranch. Julia Roberts buys houses for fun and owns about a dozen in L.A. alone. As an assistant, "the house" (guaranteed to be either Spanish, modern, or bastardized country French) can become a big focus of the job. One star's assistant spent weeks trying to bully a fountain company into changing the water's flow in the backyard. Another drove thirteen hours from L.A. to a star's vacation home in rural Arizona to deliver an antique light fixture too fragile to ship.

For the most part, an assistant's view of "the house" is relegated to two rooms: the immaculate state-of-the-art kitchen, which only the Spanish-speaking employees ever set foot in; and whatever room serves as the equivalent of the "home office." This is usually an overdone guest house with a couple of cordless phones, a pool table, and defunct gym equipment. Nonetheless, it's not such a bad lifestyle, the assistant thinks, heading back to his Geo Metro. And even the faint glimmer that someday this could be his keeps him working harder and harder.

Moving In: Life at the Bottom of the Hollywood Hills

In Xanadu did Kubla Khan
A stately pleasure dome decree
So twice five miles of fertile ground
With walls and towers were girdled round.
  —*Citizen Kane*

Los Angeles is everything a great American city should be: rich, hilarious,
of questionable taste, and throbbing with fake glamour.
  —John Waters

The cutthroat producers, the millionaire divas, the soulless executives, and the ruthless agents live like the sultans of Dubai, like the Moorish princes of Alhambra, like the lords of a million serfs. They live in Spanish mansions beyond wrought-iron gates, with great white halls striped with twenty-foot black beams and Moroccan rugs tossed across the tiles. Deep leather sofas sit beneath eighty-pound Mexican candelabras. They live in modernist Zen palaces perched atop a Hollywood hill, with walls of glass that capture a picture of Lake Hollywood in elegant rectangles, each framing fans of palm, spikes of imported bamboo, and the soft curves of the dry, silvery blue canyon. They live in Frank Lloyd Wright houses, they live in Malibu spreads that blind with whiteness and light. They roll calls around the pools, around the basement gyms. They argue plot points from an Eames chair, a Nelson bench. And at the end of the day, they take a vitamin, turn off the light. The only sound echoing throughout the house comes from the soft touch of their manicured feet making disappearing depressions on leather tiles as they head off to bed.

On the other hand, frayed assistants, stoned interns, and enthusiastic out-of-work actors live at the bottom of a Hollywood hill, or in "Beverly Hills adjacent," or beyond the canyons, in the flats. They eke out a happy life in small apartments, shared quarters with views of stucco, or a driveway, or a dilapidated pool that is green with neglect. Vista del Freeway, that's what it's like. But it's okay, there are wonderful places for the little people. Los Angeles is actually more affordable than New York and certainly comparable to other big cities. To your advantage there is a lot of space, so if you chose the right neighborhood, you can have up to four whole rooms for under a grand.

There are little bungalows in neighborhoods of varying degrees of safety and neighbors who pay far too much attention to you, "but, hey, Jean Harlow's stand-in once lived here." It's like *Melrose Place* without the flattering lighting or Jack Wagner and Heather Locklear to wake you up with nightly confrontations in the courtyard. There are sad, but private and safe apartments and there are roommate possibilities that boggle the mind. You could be living with a frustrated set designer with an eating disorder or an ambitious dog walker who recounts each morning's hikes in great detail. Or, like one actor we know, share the rent with David Schwimmer only to be dumped when he gets the role you're both up for on a new show called *Friends*.

The movie studios are scattered from Century City to Burbank, over an hour's drive in the rush, so you want to be careful to keep the commute to a minimum. It's bad enough getting to the office at eight, it's another thing to leave your house at seven, which means a daily 6 A.M. shower and speed-thru at Starbucks, which means you should be in bed at around 11 P.M., if you want to impress your boss with speed dialing and a clear vision of his or her phone sheet.

The city of Hollywood is separate from the concept of Hollywood; the geographical area of the district extends from the summit of the Hollywood Hills on the North to Beverly Boulevard on the South to Dunn Drive on the West to Hoover Street on the East. Hollywood proper is not the center of the movie business; it is, nevertheless, a neighborhood that is central, with studios bordering on three sides.

Hollywood the "community" is made up of anyone engaged in the production of motion pictures and television, but the people engaged therein live over the wide area of Los Angeles. And, as F. Scott Fitzgerald noted, "You know exactly what kind of people economically live in each section, from executives and directors, through technicians in their bungalows, right down to the extras." You want to be in a cool area but, unless you are a trust-fund brat, you won't be able to afford much and you will need a degree of safety, so that your crappy car and your college boom box won't get stolen.

These days the players are spread out as far as the eastern "suburb" of Echo Park, bordering on the various ghettos of downtown L.A., to the steeped hills of Brentwood and the lofty Pacific Palisades. Despite the endless sprawl, the hierarchy is simple. Here's the array, folks, of what you can expect:

PACIFIC PALISADES

This is an area you can expect to visit only if your world includes the likes of Goldie Hawn or Steven Spielberg. There's scant chance that you will find room and board in this posh spread of multimillion-dollar homes that mostly overlook the ocean and are mostly at the end of long driveways. Pacific Palisades, like the best of Beverly Hills, might be compared to the exclusive white sections of Johannesburg, so remote is it from "real" life. The superstars live here, for many reasons, the most noble of which is that it provides one of the best school districts in Los Angeles. It's a grown-up with kids kind of area, where the toddlers of moguls bump lunch boxes on the way to their "progressive" private schools. This is a neighborhood for those who have "really made it."

Pacific Palisades is perched nicely between the cities of Santa Monica and Malibu or between the hills and the sea. Founded in 1922 as a residential community, it has a population of about 23,000 and "the village atmosphere still exists," brags one website. There are rows of trinket shops and fake Parisian restaurants that are really quaint, but built approximately one year ago. The Palisades tries to be New England, but with some Spanish haciendas thrown in for good measure. It's your typical L.A. architectural mishmash, craftsman houses butt up against sleek moderns and because there are a lot of real estate offices, and Starbucks on every block, you could call it a certain kind of post-modern village. A village that includes chains like Noah's Bagels and It's a Wrap, so that Mr. and Mrs. Tom Hanks have somewhere to go when they leave their gated grounds.

Homes in the Palisades are high-end, well-landscaped, and often either secluded or with outstanding views. The median household income is about $102,000. As for the demographics, the only members of the city's racial minorities you'll see as you drive along Sunset Boulevard will be the ones selling maps to the stars' homes.

BRENTWOOD

You've seen Brentwood from a helicopter during the O.J. stakeout, so you may already have a picture of the massive, nouveau riche estates. Many nonmurderers live there, too, perhaps because like Pacific Palisades it means a good education for the precious kids and a safe, secluded neighborhood. Brentwood is closer to "real," with fewer flashy, expensive homes. It claims a certain modesty, but one drive through and you'll understand why the heads of agencies and lawyers make this their nest. It's country club living.

SANTA MONICA

It borders on Brentwood, it's beach living, middle class, the citizens boast a normal, healthy existence. Residents can still have their kids go to the right school. But getting in to the best parts of the neighborhood is tough. There is one street, lined with historic (almost a hundred years old!) Spanish-style houses. Anyone who has dough and drives down this street falls in love, but the owners are not selling. There is actually a waiting list for some of the houses. Ridiculous amounts of money are regularly offered. Routinely, people slip notes under the doors of these relics, which say, in a nutshell, "Let me know when you die." Architecture buffs and Old Hollywood lovers hover around like vultures to get in.

The basic logic of Santa Monica living goes like this: It's not earthquake safe—it's built on sand, it's going to fall into the ocean—but it has cleaner air.

VENICE

This is a real beach community, generally more affordable than Santa Monica or Malibu because of the noticeable, sketchy druggies and high car-theft rate. But it's also a hip and picturesque town filled with artists, good restaurants, and a world-famous beach boardwalk full of freaks on the weekends.

Venice was founded in 1905 by Abbot Kinney, a wealthy tobacco heir and real estate developer. In an attempt to re-create the atmosphere of the Italian city of Venice, Mr. Kinney conceived and constructed more than twenty miles of canals in this western counterpart. While they have nowhere near the charm of the original Venice canals, they are really something to see. Where else would such inanity increase real estate values? In 1925, Venice was annexed by the City of Los Angeles. After several decades of further development, all but a few of the canals were filled in with new construction. In 1994, restoration on the remaining canals was completed. Over the years, the Venice canal area has undergone a process of home renovation and gentrification. It is along these canals that the more expensive Venice housing is now situated, overlooking nesting ducks and homeless people.

MALIBU

This famous, ultraexpensive beach community is primarily for people who are looking for sex or who want to impress people with a stunning beach view. Johnny Carson turned heads when he bought here years ago for a whopping $9 million. Today, prices in the neighborhood of $20 million are not unheard of. Any Hollywood neophyte would quickly learn there is a big difference between Malibu proper and the Malibu Colony. The Colony, as it is known, is a gated, guarded enclave consisting of a few dozen beachfront homes belonging to the likes of David Geffen, Jim Carrey, and Cher. While this mini-neighborhood tries its best to scare away outsiders, they must contend with this pesky law that states that the sand on the beach, up to the high-tide line, is public property.

As East Coasters will quickly tell you, the whole Malibu beach craze is desperately overrated. The beach has lots of seaweed, rough surf, undertow, and cold Pacific water. Until recently, one could find any variety of plastic floating in the water. Maybe that explains why the Spielbergs summer in the Hamptons. Still, many will swear up and down that a stroll along the beach in front of the Colony is the best way to network. And in the summertime there are almost always parties happening every weekend, with guests wandering into one house and out another. Soon the marble kitchens and faux-adobe living rooms blend together. One twenty-two-year-old actor from New York ended up having drinks with Geffen and Jeffrey Katzenberg; a producer's assistant was shocked to discover a private, walled golf course in the middle of Malibu belonging to one man. Still another youngster found himself in the hallway of the heir to Neutrogena, staring at the homeowner's framed, cancelled check to the IRS for $38 million. Tasteful decorating, by Malibu standards.

BEVERLY HILLS

This is the neighborhood that many consider conservative and safe, both socially and financially. World-famous Beverly Hills is the home of movie stars, sports celebrities, and corporate moguls. Some of the most expensive homes in the Los Angeles area are tucked into the forested nooks or perched on view sites in the Santa Monica Mountains that flank the community to the north.

It is also a business district, with many pricey shops on Rodeo Drive beckoning tourists to their glass-and-gold doors. The tourists are, in fact, the biggest detriment to Beverly Hills. They screw up traffic, they take pictures in the middle of the streets, and they provide terrible eyesores, with their loud shirts, tacky shorts, and purses and cameras strapped across both shoulders. They fill the polluting tour buses that wind their way past houses that belonged to Jimmy Stewart, Lucille Ball, Rosemary Clooney, Peter Falk, Winona Ryder, and countless others. They rush out to overpriced eateries, restaurants where soaking everything in butter is mistaken for haute cuisine, hoping to catch a glance of such luminaries as Tony Curtis, James Garner, or others they might recognize from discount long-distance phone commercials.

WESTWOOD

This college town centers around the UCLA campus and boasts a convenient proximity to the major freeways and several affluent neighborhoods. Westwood's not fancy, but it's an ideal living area for assistants working on the west side of Los Angeles. There are many apartments, in addition to the quaint Mediterranean-style houses in the flats. Westwood is generally considered a safe and solid neighborhood.

HOLLYWOOD

> *Living in Hollywood is like living in a lit cigar butt.*
> —Phyllis Diller

There is nothing we can say here about the city of Hollywood that has not already been said in much more dramatic and probably derisive fashion. Yes, it is a full-on Boulevard of Broken Dreams experience: the winos, the smack addicts, the actresses-turned-hookers. But gigantic companies like Walt Disney are working quickly and efficiently to sweep the fragments from those broken dreams under the carpet, to make way for family entertainment and tourist delights. But is it really for the better to sanitize Hollywood for your protection? Was New York enriched by Disney's turning Times Square into one big, bright box office for *The Lion King*? Perhaps John Waters said it best in his book *Crackpot:*

> When you get to Hollywood, you'll know it—it looks exactly the way you've always imagined, even if you've never seen a photograph. I always head straight for Hollywood Boulevard. Old fogies like Mickey Rooney are always dumping on this little boulevard of broken dreams, calling it a cesspool and demanding a cleanup. But they miss the point. Hollywood is supposed to be trashy.

WEST HOLLYWOOD

Although world famous for its status as a gay mecca, West Hollywood is, in reality, an upper-middle-class area of young professional types and struggling artists with gym memberships and nice cars. Most of the obviously gay element has been relegated to Santa Monica Boulevard, a more extreme version of the gay ghettos in most major cities. And like most gay areas, West Hollywood has become known for its safe, clean, and gentrified streets, teaming with cafes, day spas, health food stores, and neighborhood theaters.

However, West Hollywood has its fair share of crime, particularly car theft and vandalism and hate crimes against homosexuals. One young assistant was walking just yards from the West Hollywood police station when he was attacked by a group of gay bashers, knocked unconscious, and put into a coma for weeks. The police in West Hollywood spend most of their time ticketing traffic violators and enforcing alcohol regulations on "the strip."

SILVERLAKE

Silverlake is another artsy, substantially gay neighborhood with a much less yuppie style to it. Here, bohemia is alive and well and often wearing leather. Beautiful hills dotted with Spanish-style houses surround a giant reservoir (Silverlake). Hispanic families live near Asians and everyone enjoys the eclectic mix of restaurants, galleries, thrift stores, and biker bars. For the Hollywood worker bee, the biggest drawback about Silverlake tends to be its location: very northeastern. However, it is not at all a bad commute for those working in Burbank.

LOS FELIZ

Not far from Silverlake is the charming and lush enclave of Los Feliz. Here one can get a real taste of Old Hollywood without paying west side prices. For example, director Mimi Leder purchased Charlie Chaplin's former estate for a fraction of what the land would've cost near the beach. Of course, Los Feliz is somewhat off the beaten track—unless you're headed to Koreatown or Pasadena—but the architecture is magnificent and celebrities like Tim Curry have restored the old Spanish estates with much success.

The commercial areas of Los Feliz are small, often Spanish-speaking streets of cool diners and bars and interesting antiques stores. As with almost all neighborhoods on the east side of L.A., there is a pronounced disparity between the business districts and the nearby gated estates. An ideal situation for an assistant would be to find a guest-house rental on one of these properties.

OUTPOST

For those players with cash to burn and a love of Mediterranean architecture, the neighborhood unofficially referred to as Outpost can be a great way to move out of the rat race that is the flats and into the more private Hollywood Hills. Many people living here don't want an elderly, retired existence, but they want the luxury, the great view, and the big tax break of a $2 million castle.

The winding streets of Outpost will lead you past the houses of actors like Ben Stiller and Marilu Henner, directors like Harold Becker, hip studio executives who are getting classy but who don't want to stray far from the Hollywood scene.

BURBANK

Ah, Burbank. You heard about it at the end of game shows, when the announcer would tell you where to write for tickets. You've seen it in all its concrete glory in films like *Magnolia* and *Boogie Nights*. Like much of the illustrious San Fernando Valley, Burbank is affordable, boring, smoggy, a summertime heat trap, safe, and cheap. Perhaps most important, it is one of the only L.A. neighborhoods with a Fuddruckers. And it is actually convenient if you work at Universal, NBC, Warner Bros., or Disney.

Burbank is an odd mix of Hollywood workers and real people. There are washed-up casting directors living in split-levels next to first-generation Mexican families. Ikea looms large at the base of the mountain range that borders the city. Cities like this provided fertile ground for the pyramid scams of the early nineties. For better or worse, there is something distinctly Southern Californian, emblematic really, about Burbank.

WEST LOS ANGELES

For those working at Twentieth Century Fox, it is a disheartening reality that the closest residential areas are bordered by hideous strip malls and the very generic-looking Sepulveda Boulevard area. As the name implies, West L.A. is a no-man's-land of freeway on-ramps and coffee shops. True, there are some cute residential pockets within this area, but it's generally not a preferred locale for the Hollywood assistant.

CULVER CITY

Culver City is probably best known as the home of Sony Pictures Entertainment—i.e., the Columbia/Tri-Star lot. As a residential neighborhood, Culver City is nothing to jump up and down about, but the old bakeries and warehouses and the newer modern furniture stores and progressive schools are now revitalizing what used to be a haven for crack dealers and auto repair shops. Except for its proximity to the Sony lot, the location of Culver City is not ideal for anyone in the biz, except those who want to get to the airport in a hurry.

BEL AIR

Bel Air is a ritzy bedroom community of upper-class homes, often with spectacular views of the city or the ocean. Some of these are located in secluded, wooded folds between the hills. Like the nearby communities of Beverly Hills, Brentwood, and Pacific Palisades, Bel Air features large estates and multimillion-dollar homes. The median household income in this highly desirable community is well into six figures.

While some of the more notorious Bel Air estates are completely over-the-top replicas of European chateaux or Italian castles, many Bel Air homes are authentically Californian. This is a great area to drive through in order to learn more about fifties and sixties Los Angeles architecture. Behind the snooty gates to "East" and "West" Bel Air (approximately fifty yards apart) are some fantastic examples of ranch-style Palm Springs homes and work by architects like John Lautner and Wallace Neff. But as for those starting out in the entertainment industry, chances are you will not appreciate the $20,000 per month rent that many houses here cost.

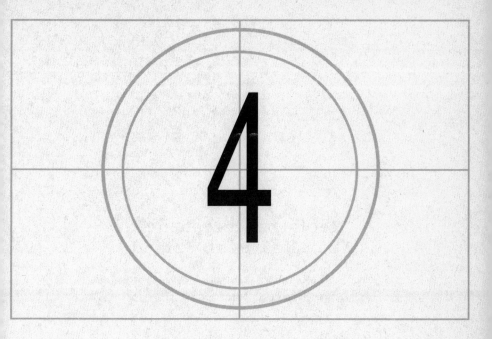

IT'S ALL YOUR FAULT! WHAT YOUR JOB REALLY ENTAILS

Meet the Telephone, Your New Best Friend

Hollywood is like being nowhere and talking to nobody about nothing.
—Michelangelo Antonioni

WHO'S WHO . . . AND WHO ISN'T

Your first task should be finding out who's who in Hollywood. And in your office. Figure out the pecking order. Chances are, everyone will have a title beginning with "VP of Creative . . ." Ask around and figure out what the hell that really means. But don't just kiss up to the big shots, it is the little people who will end up covering your back. Not to mention, everyone gets fired and promoted. Midlevel execs are in constant rotation in the entertainment industry, so don't get attached. It will only end in tears. Just know what they can do for you and get it. D-girls and D-boys are, for the most part, useful if only for the vast volumes of Hollywood scoop that passes through their headsets. Keep them happy so that you can call on them in a pinch for information about how and where to contact someone, what are a writer/director's credits, the history of a project, the status of production, or a new job opening.

The great battles of moviemaking take place over the phone, and like any war there is always an aggressor and a deflector, in other words a seller and a buyer. If you work for an agent, manager, or producer, you are always trying to get people on the phone, trying to track down your boss, make the call happen. If you work for a buyer, a studio executive, you're deflecting everyone all day.

Generally that is how it works; however, if there's a bidding war going on with a script, suddenly the studio executive wants the agent and suddenly the agent is unreachable. It's all about where the balance of power lies.

PANIC ATTACK ON LINE TWO

Now you're answering the phones and if you have read this book, you will have memorized everyone in your boss's life, from Ziva the masseuse to Lenny the business manager. However, should you be caught off guard with a new name, we will teach you how to figure it out in sixty seconds or less.

Every assistant should have:

- *The Hollywood Creative Directory* (it lists the current staff and contact information about all of the major studios, management, and production companies)
- *The Agents and Managers Directory* (similar, but extensively covering the agencies)
- *IMDB* (Internet Movie Database, an online service for researching movie credits)
- *The Writers and Directors Guild Directories* (listings of writers and directors, their representatives: lawyer, manager, agent, and their credits)
- A meticulously updated *Rolodex*, preferably on computer for speed
- *The Videohound's Golden Movie Retriever* (no conversation takes place in Hollywood without at least one, "What'd they do again?")
- *Agency Client Lists* (agencies really protect these but there are some floating around and if you can dupe a copy, you'll be in good with

your boss, who will then have a shortcut to anticipating every
agency's packaging scheme)
- *Old phone logs* (hugely important, because your boss will suddenly
  remember someone he once talked to and now needs, but he'll have
  no idea where the person works or even lives. A shortcut is to
  retrace the steps)
- Your boss's *Filofax* (at least a recent xerox of it)

. . . and the intercom extension of the old battle-ax in your
office who's been there forever and can tell you exactly who's who.

Remember, time is of the essence on all phone calls, so you
should be prepared to check all of the above simultaneously . . .
and without moving.

YOUR MASTER'S IN TELECOMMUNICATION

Speaking of telephones, they are a world unto themselves. If you
do not learn them within your first hour on the job, you might as
well start packing up and head back to your rent-a-car. Unique to
Hollywood is the notion of assistants listening in on practically
every call and jotting down key information, ready to interject at a
moment's notice. You are essentially the air-traffic controller for a
fleet of neurotic nitwits afraid of losing their status on the runway.

Hence, numerous pitfalls await you if you do not master
things like the mute button, the headset, the speed dial, the
Amtel, conference calling, transfer, and voice mail options. And,
of course, God forbid you lose a message. People have been
killed for less.

Once you've mastered the technology, you need to learn the
nuances of dealing with the people on the other end of the phone.
Prioritize calls (who's who, long-distance vs. cell phone, your
boss's boss vs. his mother), politely ask who the hell someone is,
lie efficiently for your boss, learn 250 different ways to say "we'll
call back," and know when to jump into the conversation to save

your boss. As you will see, an assistant needs to know much more than how to pick up a receiver.

ROLLING, ROLLING, ROLLING

Now, we can't in good conscience send you into your lower-level, unreserved parking space without discussing the phenomenon that has taken over the entertainment industry: rolling calls. This consists of your boss in an outside location (car, Spago, airplane, on set, chiropractor, etc.) and you placing his calls from the office while he waits by his cell phone. You also listen in on the calls, so that if he needs you for something you can jump in with dates: "Yes, you're free on the tenth"; directions: "Pass the John Wayne mural, it's in the Rita Hayworth Commissary"; or giving him synopses of scripts he can't remember: "It's that family piece about the orphan monkey and the crippled kid."

You should be well versed in the following crucial topics:

THE PHONE LOG: YES, IT CAN BE USED AS A FLOTATION DEVICE

You've heard of the shroud of Turin, the cloth carrying the image of Jesus after he was buried? Well, your phone log is more important. Forget the little pink "While You Were Out" messages and Post-its stuck to the coffee machine. Every single call, in or out, must be documented in one place. Whether saved in the computer or scrawled on the pages of a spiral phone log, all names and numbers, times of calls, and if necessary even brief messages, must be in one place, clearly recorded and accessible.

IT'S A RACE: WHO TO CALL FIRST?

Don't just start going down the list blindly, think ahead. If your boss is waiting for a response on a project that he has submitted to the studio, place the call to the executive first so that when you call the writer, your boss has an answer ready when asked, "What did the studio think?" On a personal level, don't put your boss through to his or her significant other until you have confirmed that night's dinner reservation. Figure out a method, "A" calls vs. "B" calls, "high" calls vs. "low" calls, whatever. It's not brain surgery, just be ready with the important calls first.

NO BUTTER FINGERS: A MOIST TOWELETTE CAN SAVE YOUR JOB

If you're rolling calls, time is always of the essence. Your control-freak boss is waiting in fiber-optic limbo, probably timing how long you're leaving him there. So make life easier on yourself . . . cut the nails, program the speed dial, memorize all key numbers, and wipe the phone down with HandiWipes every few hours.

THE ART OF TRANSFERENCE: LEAVING WORD FOR HALF OF ICM OR PARAMOUNT IN ONE PHONE CALL

Often you will be calling many extensions at the same studio, agency, etc. So make the assistants at these companies work for you. After leaving word for one agent, for example, ask the assistant to transfer you to the next. Continue until you've completed all the calls to that company. Why redial? The glorified version of this, perfected by one producer's assistants, consists of phoning the after-hours answering service for the larger companies and simply asking the operator to "leave word" in all of the different mailboxes. Forty messages, one phone call. If you can read a grocery list, you've got a new shortcut at your disposal.

CUTTING TO THE CHASE: THREE WORDS YOU MUST MEMORIZE

There is a sacred, time-tested formula for asking the office you are calling to take a message for the person you are trying to reach. Don't try to be cute, don't to try to expand upon or change it. Others have gone before you and failed. Just memorize this ingeniously economical phrase: "Please leave word."

Inevitably you will encounter your nemesis: the decaffeinated assistant (most likely a middle-aged, Linda Tripp knock-off from the Valley who has no desire or hope for career advancement). This is how it will happen: your boss is running late and calling from his cell phone as he drives into a canyon and you have eighty-six calls to return. On call number two you encounter the decaffeinated assistant, the telephonic equivalent of a four-car pileup on the 101 Freeway. You will be able to identify the decaf assistant by the following opening phrase: "Um, you know what, he was just here a second ago, but I think he went down the hall into a meeting, unless he's in the men's room, but if you'll hold on a second I'll just . . ." At this point, you should panic and either disconnect immediately or, if you're feeling lucky, try to interrupt Linda Tripp with some version of the three magical words: "That's okay, please leave word." Hang up before Linda can respond, and on to the next call.

I'M LOSING YOU: DEALING WITH CELL PHONES

Just like standing in line at the DMV, cellular phones are a necessary evil that you must learn to live with. They will always fuzz out at the crucial moments and they will never work in the areas that your boss commutes to and from. But no matter your frustration level, your duty is to redial every time your boss or whomever he's talking to disconnects. Occasionally, this technological sham can be used to your advantage; for example, an assistant to one of the senior agents at William Morris would frequently cut off her boss midtantrum by rubbing her headset against her desktop, creating "interference." Clichéd perhaps, but effective. Your boss can also benefit, if you inadvertently reach someone your boss didn't really want to connect with. "He was in the car, I just lost him" is a phrase you should become quite comfortable with. To enhance your credibility, memorize the names of all canyons and tunnels in the L.A. area.

LEAVING WORD AT MIDNIGHT: THE ART OF NEVER GETTING SOMEONE ON THE PHONE

Hollywood etiquette and cowardice dictate that every call be returned within about twenty-four hours. In the words of Motion Picture President Jack Valenti, "The single most important piece of advice I can give anyone in the movie business is to return every phone call." But if you are working for a "buyer," your boss will be besieged by calls he's really not that excited to return. Welcome to the wonderful world of "call dumping." This is where you can use the law of Hollywood scheduling to your advantage. Offices open at 9 A.M. (although most players can be successfully not reached until 9:30 A.M.); lunch is from 1 to 2:30ish and it's easy to miss someone by calling after 7 P.M. or on weekends. Hence, by counterposing your schedule to the rest of the 323 and 310 area code members, you can successfully avoid a call for months, giving the caller enough time to have forgotten about the "Untitled Kelsey Grammer" vehicle he submitted to your boss.

HOLLYWOOD 911:
WHEN TO USE THE WORD "URGENT"

The new assistant would be wise to discuss the use of the word "urgent," and what qualifies as urgent, early on. Though to the novice it may seem obvious when an emergency arises, many of you will not realize just what might happen when a hard-to-reach hotel concierge calls to leave a message about a suite change. Conversely, many callers will announce their call as "urgent" as a means to get by you. After all, you're the bouncer with the list at the velvet rope. Take heed and run each of these pronouncements through your "urgency filter" before pulling your boss out of a "production meeting" (Latin for "high colonic").

Here's an example to learn from: An assistant to a literary agent once interrupted a staff meeting of all the literary agents to say, "Claudia Eller is calling, she says it's urgent." Between gritted teeth, the agent uttered, "Call back." After the meeting the assistant found out, behind closed doors and from the mouth of his red-faced, enraged boss, that Claudia Eller was the gossip columnist for *Variety*, and he had just been exposed in front of all of his colleagues as the guy who had been leaking details of confidential deals in order to promote himself.

THE OATH OF OFFICE: HOW TO LIE
COMFORTABLY IN AN UNCOMFORTABLE HEADSET

In addition to the white lies discussed above, such as the cellular canyon lie and the "in a production meeting" excuse, there are several more Clintonian phrases that it would behoove any assistant to memorize:

"He's on the set with his phone off."

"He's locked in an editing room."

"He's on a looping stage, trying to get Patrick Swayze to lose his accent."

"He's stuck in a last-minute production rewrite meeting with a hostile writer."

"He's in an all-day read-though."

"He's been on the phone with Washington all morning, begging for a PG-13."

"I know he's anxious to speak to you."

"I wasn't on that call."

Again, we're not encouraging dishonesty in the workplace, but your boss undoubtedly will, so it's best to be prepared.

ALL CALLS ARE NOT CREATED EQUAL: "MICHAEL OVITZ CALLING" VS. "MICHAEL OVITZ'S OFFICE CALLING"

Case in point: In an effort to update Bill's Rolodex, Ceridwen called Michael Ovitz's office to confirm some information. Naturally, she gets voice mail and leaves a message. Days later, when the call is returned, Ceridwen hears "Michael Ovitz's office on line three" and races into the conference room, interrupting a writer who is in midpitch to drag Bill out for the "urgent call." Bill picks up to find Ovitz's impatient assistant waiting to give anyone with a pen their new fax number. Why not learn from her mistakes and verify who *exactly* is calling for whom.

MULTITASKING:
TWO PHONES ARE BETTER THAN ONE

If you have a hope in hell of actually getting your job done while glued to your boss's calls all day, you must learn the art of the multiphone shuffle. Traditionally, this is done whilst on headset on one phone, where you roll calls and vaguely listen in on your boss's chitchat, simultaneously using another phone to make the calls you need to complete your daily tasks. This treacherous endeavor involves significant ear-mouth coordination skills and a dexterous finger on the mute button. In essence, you will need to be able to carry on one conversation while eavesdropping on another. You will sing, "please hold" as a chorus between the verses of your two conversations. Your goal is to get your boss on a call as quickly as possible, in order to enhance your own phone time.

CALL ME EVERY FIVE MINUTES: THE HOLLYWOOD LINGO

Meet every assistant's alter ego: Rolanda Calls. Rolanda only speaks in Hollywoodspeak: "Per our conversation," "I look forward to hearing your thoughts," "touching base," "face-to-face," "in bed with you," "on board," "on the same page," "in the same room," "on the same train," "going in the same direction," "hip and edgy," "let's put it in the books right now"; and like everyone she overhears in Hollywood, Rolanda is very "passionate" about her job.

Rolanda will tell you, language in Hollywood has its own set of rules. Everyone says, "you and I" even when it's supposed to be "you and me." "Let's get him in a room with you and I and we'll see if we're on the same page." Are industry folks stupid or are they just afraid of using the word "me"? Either way, it doesn't matter because if everyone is making the same mistake, it becomes the norm, so embrace it.

"BURBANK, WE HAVE A PROBLEM": THE HOLLYWOOD CONFERENCE CALL

It all sounds so simple: a call needs to be scheduled between the studio head, the VP of production, the creative exec, the story editor, and the producer. Easy, right? Get together times from the studio representatives and then call the producer with options. This is what one perky, newly hired assistant to a studio executive did. Well, when she reached the producer's assistant (this producer, by the way, was one of those powerhouse, shoot-'em-up, phallic fantasy, action producers), she cheerfully offered times for the call. The assistant responded, "Um, can you hold on a sec?" Our happy assistant waited for the response and she got it, but not from the assistant. The producer himself got on the line and screamed, "You called me last?! Who is this? What the f**k were you thinking? You're giving me dates? I'll give *you* the dates!"

The assistant choked out an apology, then hung up and burst into tears. When her boss, the VP of production, arrived some minutes later to see her tear-streaked cheeks, he asked for the story. Lucky for this girl, her boss was extremely sympathetic. So was the head of the studio, who felt so bad about this incident that he personally came down to her office and apologized on behalf of the producer. The good news: She went on to become the assistant to this studio head and currently makes a living as a VP at his company.

Don't Look a Gift Basket
in the Mouth

You can take all the sincerity in Hollywood, place it in the navel of a fruit fly and still have room enough for three caraway seeds and a producer's heart.

—Fred Allen

Christmas and birthdays are just two occasions for gift giving in the entertainment industry. But what about these: starting or wrapping film production, sealing a deal, receiving an award nomination, receiving an award, signing with a new agency, buying a new house, a hernia operation, etc. As an assistant, you will be asked to come up with a brilliant, memorable gift for each occasion. One that doesn't come in a basket.

Hollywood loves to "show it" rather than "say it." After all, this is the business of entertainment where dramatic physical and visual gestures pack a bigger punch than the spoken or written word. It's not so much about the value of a gift as it is about the creativity involved. The "fruit basket" in Hollywood often delivers no fruit, but rather such diverse things as Slinkies, homeopathic remedies, books, slippers, whiskey, sunscreen, bath crystals, disposable cameras, etc. One writer was hand delivered ten pounds of ice-packed Chilean sea bass from a producer who knew that the writer was on a diet.

Places like Hardtoshopfor.com are cropping up, specializing in start-of-production gifts, wrap gifts, and "original baskets for all occasions." But, in the end, these helpful consumer guides read like an in-flight shopping mall, with typical offerings for the man who has it all: portable, vibrating body massagers; kick 'n' pull pool weights; a scheduler–Rolodex–alarm clock–word processor all in a handy unit the size of a shirt button. So to really impress, "think outside the box," put down the Sharper Image catalogue, and call the recipient's assistant and ask about his boss. Assistants have an understanding about these things. They'll give you insider scoop on their boss's interests, yet you still may get the usual "golf," "black-and-white photography," or "red wine" response.

But even from those generic responses you can still be creative. For example, one assistant to a producer discovered in conversations with a colleague's assistant that the colleague (an Academy Award winner) was obsessed with dogs. Who isn't, in Hollywood? What could this bland nugget of information possibly inspire? Well, the clever assistant remembered discovering a tiny booth in a multiplex of antique stores in New York (Twenty-third Street, to be exact) where an eccentric woman will send a photograph of your dog to an elderly, British dog painter, who lives in the Cotswolds. Within four months this old master will whip up a magnificent, miniature oil painting of your beloved pet (now, of course, pictured on a bed of moss, with rolling highlands in the distance) for approximately $400 (peanuts to any self-respecting Hollywood hotshot). Brochure in hand, four months before Christmas, this assistant hips her boss to the "classic, British dog painter" and the boss flips. "Not only is it great because of the dogs, but she also collects kitsch artwork and thrift store paintings, this is perfect!" He had the assistant work in cahoots with his colleague's housekeeper to get the photograph and the next thing you know the stunning portrait is being unveiled at an intimate dinner party with about two dozen dog-loving superstars. They gasped with jealousy. "How did you find out about this?!?!" Our guess is he gave himself the credit.

But by now you should know, it's not about getting credit, it's about making your boss look like a thoughtful, brilliant, widely informed, punctual person of impeccable taste and timing.

Of course, knowing exactly what the gift recipient "loves" doesn't necessarily always work. A certain movie star who shall remain nameless but who has been written up in style magazines around the world, was once given, by her high-powered agent, a designer handbag. She laughed aloud upon opening this $1,500 present. "What does my agent's assistant know about style?!?!" She tossed the purse aside.

The lesson: Be aware of the gift getter's interests but don't attempt to find Robert Redford the perfect palomino or Woody Allen the hippest jazz CD. So if personal interests don't work, go for clever and funny. For example, when Barry Diller bought Polygram Films, a certain director, whose deal was being inherited by Diller, wanted to send the perfect congratulatory gift. In a brilliant example of resourcefulness, the assistant sent Mr. Diller a flower arrangement containing a pair of sterling silver handcuffs in the center, accompanied by a simple note reading, "You're stuck with me now." Indeed, the gift had the intended effect, as evidenced by the note that came back a few days later: "Stuck is good . . . Barry."

There are the lavish exceptions to the moderately priced gifts (i.e., below $1,000) that are circulated. The helmers at Warner Bros. shelled out over half a million bucks in the form of eight brand-new Range Rovers for the A-list talent on *Lethal Weapon 3* when the first weekend's box office receipts hit their desks.

This kind of excess can trickle down to you, on the rare occasion. A creative executive tells us that when he worked for a notoriously tough producer, he was rewarded with a top-of-the-line laser disc player for his birthday and a digital camera as a departure gift. Another assistant received a new queen-size bed from her generous boss, for no reason other than he felt sorry for her, having just moved to L.A. and sleeping on her college futon. When she received the bed she called to thank him; his reply: "You'll need to be well-rested for this job, trust me."

Rumor has it that such like-minded movie stars as Charlie Sheen and Emma Thompson both presented their hard-working assistants with expensive cars. But for the most part you'll be lucky to take home one of the many awful gifts your boss has no use for: candles, tinned crumb cakes, colorful bins of caramel popcorn, solid chocolate cell phones, hastily inscribed hardcover copies of such mass-marketed, spiritual guides as *The Art of War* and *Don't Sweat the Small Stuff* or children's books with a message we can still learn from, like *The Giving Tree;* and of course, endless hats, Ts, tanks, totes all emblazoned with slogans for whatever recent studio bomb your boss just sunk with. Not to mention the piles of discarded premiere baggies filled with luxury items like Dr. Marten's shoe polishing kits, Revlon auburn glow conditioner, Revlon smudge-proof eye crayons, Revlon everything (Ron Perelman just can't say no to the word "cosponsor"). After all, what does Christian Slater need with an umbrella and raincoat set reminding him, in Day-Glo lettering, of his adventurous decision to go "action" in *Hard Rain?* And the soundtrack? It's yours. If you work for someone who has the consideration to save all the junket crap for some poor soul, like the new-to-Hollywood assistant, you'll be living large in logos and entertaining your friends to the tune of the *My Giant* soundtrack.

The Art of the Meeting

The nice thing about being a celebrity is that when you bore people, they think it's their fault.

—Henry Kissinger

Most of the business we call "show" takes place behind closed doors in the all-important "meeting." The meeting is critical, it is the forum where everything happens, decisions are made, talent is heard, plots are reworked, budgets are granted. The meeting is where relationships are made or broken, agents and clients are hired or fired, TV series are sold or killed, and the verdict is passed on a star's hairstyle. Huge judgment calls are made in these meetings, judgments that can have far-reaching effects on the course of entertainment history. And nowhere is the assistant more instrumental than in the planning, confirming, and note-taking of the Hollywood meeting.

Sally Assistant has been on the phone all day trying to arrange a meeting between a hot, young actress (most recently seen on the cover of *People*'s "too thin" issue), an effeminate British director (whose claim to fame was an award-winning short film that nobody actually watched), a highly paid screenwriter (never had a film produced), and Sally's boss, the schmoozy producer of the project they're all going to do together.

The purpose of the meeting is for the actress to give her notes on the script to the writer, with the supervision and approval of the director and producer. Simple enough, it would seem. Except that everything in Hollywood is political and every meeting is a pain in the ass, particularly for Sally Assistant.

She's been calling the skinny star's agent's assistant's voice mail all day to find out when this goddess from the San Fernando Valley can make it to the venerable Sony Pictures lot in scenic Culver City. Finally she gets an answer: "Call her publicist." Skinny, it seems, is doing a photo shoot for the cover of the substantive literary magazine *Jane*, and so her schedule for the day has been taken over by her publicist's office—sort of like when the space shuttle goes from ground control to satellite radar. Once the publicist's assistant nails down a time that Skinny is free ("She'll have plenty of time during lunch, since it seems she won't be eating"), Sally Assistant dutifully notifies the director, writer, and her boss, the producer. Meeting's set, case closed, right?

Not so fast. The British director is terribly hungover in his suite at a West Hollywood hotel, where someone named Jacques keeps answering the phone in his room, demanding to know if Sally is the person they paged at 4 A.M. at the behest of Carlos, the bartender at the Manhole. After Sally explains she really has no idea where to get hold of crystal meth on such short notice, she gets the message about the 1 P.M. meeting to the director.

The writer, of course, is available. He's at home, of course, and answers the phone because he'd rather do anything other than write. Of course he'll come in for a meeting at lunchtime because A) he won't actually be able to write while he's in a meeting; and B) there's a free meal involved. So Sally's now completed her task, right? Wrong. The writer wants to know which gate his drive-on pass will be for. It better be the fancy main entrance, near the executive parking lot, not the huge parking superstructure that resembles Alcatraz. And does he have a reserved space? Good. Which one? Could he get a closer space? "And what's for lunch, by the way? Ordering in? From where? Why not the Ivy? No, they do deliver if you use the gourmet delivery service. Well, then send an intern. Jeez. And make sure there are some vegetarian dishes. And I'm lactose intolerant. Oh, one more thing, can I bring my dog?"

This all occurs while Sally is frantically searching for the number of the real estate agent with whom her boss was going to look at Malibu beach houses at lunchtime, until he remembered he forgot to tell Sally to cancel until just now.

One P.M. Sally schleps into the conference room with eight bags of food from the Ivy. "I'm not eating," Skinny offers helpfully from the corner couch, where she's curled up flipping through *In Style* magazine's riveting account of why Val Kilmer's so misunderstood. The writer, clad in a black T-shirt and Barneys black leather jacket because it's the law, starts pawing through the bags of food, dropping assorted entrées into the waiting mouth of his Australian shepherd puppy, Mel. "Technically, these crab cakes aren't vegetarian, Sally." She can't hear him, though, from under the table where the coffeemaker has broken into a million pieces, thanks to the shaky hands of the hungover director. "I can fix it," offers Sally from the floor. "How fast?" the director asks.

The producer comes in, demanding to know if he has any new calls and why has Sally not fetched everyone their preferred beverage. Before she can answer, not that she would because Sally is a pro who knows that assistants are guilty until proven guilty, the producer tells her he wants detailed notes taken of the ensuing meeting. Although she briefly wonders what she'll do about her Honda hatchback still double-parked in the fire lane in front of the building, engine running, she nods and grabs a steno pad with one hand and a bottle of sparkling water for Skinny with the other.

Let the meeting begin.

These meetings generally consist of about ten minutes of preliminary chitchat, followed by about thirty minutes of actual exchanging of ideas. The meeting then concludes with five minutes of reassuring remarks about what a great meeting it was and

how everyone is now "on the same page" and things are just
dandy. Then everyone leaves, secretly enraged that they didn't get
everything they wanted and were forced to compromise. The
writer and director call their agents and scream about the lack of
respect with which they are treated. The actress worries about
why she's working with these people. The producer hates them
all, knows what they're all thinking, but is just glad he's lived to
fight another day.

During the preliminary chitchat section, Sally Assistant generally keeps her mouth shut, since no one cares about schmoozing
or exchanging pleasantries with the help. This time is really a
warm-up period for the players to feel one another out, discover
what kind of moods they're in, and impress one another with
what they did over the weekend. Inevitably Sally will have to suffer through recitations of the pros and cons of Brentwood real
estate, replete with pressing dilemmas like: "Sunset Boulevard—
to be north or south of it?" or "Why is it so hard to find an
authentic Spanish hacienda in Santa Monica?" And, of course, an
all-time favorite: "Do you know how much David Geffen spent
on Jack Warner's old estate?"

After real estate gossip is exchanged (a thinly veiled way for
insiders to discuss how much everyone's worth), the writer will
generally try and impress the group with one or two culturally
significant things he's done lately. Perhaps he's seen one of the
two mediocre theater productions in L.A. Or the Met's leftovers
on display at the L.A. County Museum of Art. More likely, he's
gone to a fund-raiser for the Venice Family Clinic and feels really
great about having contributed a hundred bucks in exchange for a
bunch of Christmas cards he can send out, trumpeting, "A contri-
bution has been made in your name . . ."

But as the meeting begins in earnest, generally by the producer
clearing his throat loudly and ungracefully segueing into the work
at hand, Sally must snap to attention. She is expected to take
detailed notes, dutifully recording the ideas laid out and who's
saying what. This will allow her producer boss to later brief the

studio on what direction the script will be taking. More important, it will allow her boss to claim credit for most of the ideas presented, until the studio shoots them down, at which point he will disavow them.

Since it is a scientifically proven fact that no one in Hollywood can concentrate on one subject for more than half an hour at a time, Sally Assistant will often be asked to freshen drinks or help serve lunch. This provides a chance for bathroom breaks and Sally can check all the messages piling up on her desk. It is important to note that an assistant's sitting in on a meeting is considered a privilege and does not serve as an excuse to drop the ball on any other responsibilities.

As the meeting winds down, the assistant might get a chance to utter a few words, usually along the lines of "Nice to meet you," or "Can I get your coat?" The players, meanwhile, shake hands and exchange empty promises to "be in touch soon," "call with any questions," etc. Sally now has the daunting task of deciphering many legal pad pages of her own hurried scrawl, and typing up the official "meeting notes" to give to her boss, pronto.

What often happens within a few hours, or perhaps a day or two, is that everyone involved comes to realize they didn't get enough accomplished and they need to have another meeting. The writer has questions, as always. "The writer has questions," by the way, is a Hollywood euphemism for "the overpaid guy in the black leather jacket is really pissed he has to do more work and might threaten to walk off the project if we don't hold his hand while he has a temper tantrum about the fact that no one thinks as highly of his perfectly constructed scene as he does."

Chances are that Sally might actually glean these details before anyone else. How? It is a well-known fact that upwardly mobile assistants and screenwriters frequent the same hangouts. Why? Because the writers (generally male and wealthier than they are attractive) find better mating odds with the assistants (generally female and more attractive than they are wealthy). So Sally probably heard the writer in the black jacket, or one of his friends, cry-ing into their cosmopolitan about the outrageous castration the screenplay has undergone at the hands of Skinny the actress. Since Sally is a good assistant, she will not breathe a word of this to anyone, nor will she act hurt when the writer breezes into the office next time and ignores her, not giving her so much as a "hello" as she hands him his Diet Peach Snapple iced tea.

However, should the writer reveal anything that might be useful to Sally's boss, Sally will of course give the producer a heads-up, if only to cover her own ass when the writer says, "But I told Sally I wasn't going to change the opening scene to a helicopter shot of downtown L.A."

But none of that is as important as catching key phrases actually uttered during these meetings. If, on rare occasion, a producer actually has a good creative idea to contribute, woe be to the assistant who neglects to jot it down. Yes, there is a lot of vamping in these meetings, so how does one know when to actually pay attention as an idea heads down the tracks? Well, one disingenuous phrase that should perk up the ears of any assistant is, "This is probably a bad idea, but . . ." This phrase translates loosely to: "Here's what better be in the next rewrite or we're hiring Carrie Fisher." Another classic is, "I'm not a writer, so you tell me, but I was thinking . . ." This, of course, is passive-aggressive speak for, "Look, I can have a better idea off the top of my head than you've had during the last six months, and you're the one being paid the gross national product of Luxembourg." Similarly, the smart assistant will always write down whatever follows these lead-ins:

Lead-in: Do you know which scene keeps haunting me from the old draft?

Translation: We should have kept the original writer, but since we didn't, could you at least try to copy his style?

Lead-in: Guess what my teenage daughter's friends told me they really love to see in a movie?

Translation: Our target demographic wants a happy ending, not some tearful flashback to childhood.

Lead-in: The craziest idea popped into my head driving to work today . . .

Translation: The studio called and they want Jennifer Love Hewitt.

Lead-in: I hate to give such a Hollywood studio note, but . . .

Translation: If you think we're going to spend $75 million on a movie where Tom Cruise's character doesn't get laid, you're fucking insane.

Lead-in: What do we all think of scene number . . . ?

Translation: Who wants to keep their job? Good, tell the writer to get rid of this.

Lead-in: As a nonwriter I'll give a lame example, and this is only to spark more ideas, but the bad way to do that might be to . . .

Translation: Write what I am about to say into the script, verbatim.

After a couple of these "creative meetings," most assistants get the hang of it. After all, as with so many things Hollywood, the general rules of hypocrisy, cowardice, deception, control, and cruelty apply.

No matter how high on the Hollywood ladder one climbs, one will often have to explain one's very important creative ideas to a little black box: the speaker phone. As an assistant, you will witness the madness of this form of communication firsthand. What follows is a heartbreaker, a typical scenario in the moviemaking workplace, and the kind of experience particularly depressing for assistants who dream of a glamorous screenwriting career.

Here's the scene: A writer enters the offices of what we'll call TriMax. He is led by an assistant to a sparse, dim room with no windows and a long, empty boardroom table surrounded by six chairs. In the center of the table sits the most important member of the meeting: one of those big, complicated phones with a flat speaker that, from the writer's POV, seems to suck all the heat, light, and warmth from the room into its unforgiving silence. The writer takes a seat, the notes for his "take" on a "concept" shaking in his hand. In comes the assistant with the Snapple, then the D-girl (whom the writer recognizes as a former waitress from a French bistro where he used to eat last year when he was unem-

ployed) sits across from the writer and asks questions about whatever holiday just passed, and they share thoughts on East Coast
versus West Coast—"It really is so boring in L.A., all I do is
work, God, but it's totally good though"—and then another guy
comes in. The writer is introduced to him quickly, it's unclear
what he does, the D-girl simply says, "John is going to be sitting
in on the call" and then John leans back in his chair and smiles a
very cheap smile at the writer, who can only think, This guy's outfit cost more than I made on my last "polish," but is interrupted
from this important realization by the assistant, who stands at the
door: "Okay, New York is on line four, you guys can jump on."

The D-girl presses a button and then leans into the phone and
speaks, as if to a foreigner, loudly and elongated, "Hi, we're all
on!" Hellos are clumsily exchanged, each one on top of the next,
and then the studio president, whom we can refer to as "Charlie,"
complains about a back problem or a stomach flu, or some weird
physical malady that is somehow supposed to make the writer feel
that there is a human on the other end of this cord, and then
there's a funny silence, which is not at all funny to the writer, who
knows he has to walk to the end of the diving board and jump.
"Okay, so I guess I'll just dive right in." "Yeah, dive right in,"
someone agrees.

Ten minutes later, no one else has said anything, the writer is
furiously describing the "set piece," failing to make the little gags
he rehearsed the night before sound spontaneous, when suddenly
Charlie interrupts, "Can you change the character's name from
Gary? Gary always seems like a creepy name to me." This completely disrupts the flow of the writer's "take" and so he wraps it up
faster than he can count the fillings in the teeth of the expensive-
suit guy's mouth each time he yawns. The D-girl thanks the writer,
the expensive suit spiels a few arrogant paragraphs about what
"kind of movie" this is, with most sentences ending with "per se,"
"as it were," and "if you will." The studio president says they have
to "jump" but "thanks," "thanks," "thanks" and the writer is ushered
back to the reception area for parking "validation."

In his car it starts again: the talking into thin air, this time between him and his "hands-free" cell phone kit. His agent "jumps on" and says, "Well, they said you put a lot of work into it," which is a well-known Hollywood euphemism, for "they hated it."

Meanwhile, the other side of this story is what you get to see if you are the New York assistant: specifically, the studio prez, with his finger on the mute button after the first two minutes of the pitch, asking you some important question like, "Do you really think I've lost weight?" and then, after a few more minutes of not listening, ordering you to get lunch and then, at the end of the pitch, needing you to literally nudge him awake to respond.

How to (Not) Read a Script

You call this a script? Give me a couple of five-thousand-dollar-a-week writers and I'll write it myself.

— Joe Pasternak, producer

Depending on the job, you may be asked to read screenplays. Even if you're not asked to, it can be impressive and helpful to your boss if you know what's going on in your company and you can offer yourself up. Be aware, though, that if you are a willing and smart reader, they will pile on the scripts with no extra pay. But for many, this can be the most interesting part of the job.

Like so many things in Hollywood, as in life, what you really want is usually not what you get. Those assistants who have a genuine passion for reading new material rarely get to take home any good screenplays (the D-girls and D-boys have them poolside in their West L.A. Spanish-style sublets). Inevitably those who are not really interested in (or talented at) reading and evaluating material are loaded up with the office's excess submissions. You prefer comedies? No one cares, here's the first draft of a Ashley Judd vehicle. You majored in comparative literature in school and really want to write coverage on novels? Great, you can let us know your thoughts on *The Cat in the Hat* for Jim Carrey. And that's if you're a highly regarded assistant at Dream-

Works. Imagine the choice sirloin available in the Dimension Films library.

Also, keep in mind that even those employers who may want help with their reading load may be hesitant to trust their three-hole-punched treasures to you. After all, taste in writing, as in movies, can vary widely and getting to know your colleagues' predilections takes time. So when you're sitting across that desk during your interview explaining how you really, really want to read scripts in your spare time because your ultimate goal is to produce (or write, or direct), don't be surprised by the tepid response from el bosserooni because: A) he's probably already hired someone who's supposed to be doing that for him; B) he can get better coverage faxed to him from studio story departments or agencies; and C) who the hell are you kidding that you'll have spare time?

Perhaps we're overstating the situation to make our point. The fact is, there are small companies who let assistants contribute to discussions of potential material, writers, and filmmakers. Hell, there are even potential bosses out there who will read your shelf full of lousy screenplays you've been writing since that college film class you took, the one taught by some coassociate producer of *Butch Cassidy*.

When you do have the opportunity to contribute creatively, or at least editorially, you should be prepared to impress. Some advice: Keep it simple. Limit your analysis to character, dialogue, plot, and story structure. Many wannabe development assistants make the mistake of offering up their opinions about what budget range a script falls into or if it's a "big movie" or an "art house film." Save it. If Tom Hanks does it, it's a big movie—get it? If Sean Penn or Ed Burns does it, it's not.

To contribute to your boss's or coworkers' agenda, you must know what they're looking for in new material. This information can help you eliminate a lot of bad or inappropriate scripts by page 20. Which leads us to the "ten-minute trick." See, by this point in your fledgling career, you're working grueling fourteen-hour days and you sleep all weekend. Suddenly, that stack of 120-page screenplays next to your futon seems less compelling than when you sat in the CAA human resources office just dying for a chance to get your Gucci loafers in the door. You need a short-cut . . . the ten-minute trick, or the "quick twenty," as it is known among those who sit in the worst seats at premieres. This simple idea can help you knock off a script in a pinch.

THE QUICK TWENTY: CLIFFS NOTES, HOLLYWOOD STYLE

Since the established screenplay formula dictates that the charac-ters, plot setup, and inciting incident should occur by about page 21, you may read the first act, then a few pages around page 60 (the midpoint where subplots are supposed to converge), and then the final five to ten pages. Theoretically, you will now have a pretty good idea of the writer's ear for dialogue, a working knowl-edge of the main characters, and the plot setup and payoff. At least enough to know if you are dealing with an engaging piece that might merit closer attention. This trick can save you hours.

Intuition can be another great timesaver. There are certain tell-tale signs that many bad scripts share. For example, if the leading male character is named JAKE, run for the hills. If the leading female character has a traditionally male name (as in, "We pull back from the alarm clock to reveal the voluptuous silhouette of JOHNNY, an angel with a dirty face and a 9mm Glock in hand"), head toward the recycling bin. In fact, anytime you see the word "Glock" or "sawed-off shotgun" within the first five pages of a script, your hack-o-meter should be buzzing. Woody Allen once noted his favorite hackneyed description line that he felt best summed up all bad screenwriting: " . . . his face, an ashen mask." Other giveaways include phrases like:

"The door opens on SAM, a Julia Roberts type."

"JACK, early thirties, ruggedly handsome."

"Despite the volcanic soot, we can tell she's naturally beautiful."

"Cut to: INT. OVAL OFFICE—11:59 P.M."

"Her rumpled waitress uniform belies her unkempt beauty."

" . . . unaware of his boyish good looks."

"I am the president of the United States."

"The kind of town Norman Rockwell would love."

"They move together, rhythmically, their passion reaching a crescendo."

We know, we know. You think we're being so terribly unfair to the writer. The artist. The talent. Whatever. The fact is that 99 percent of all scripts logged by agencies, studios, and production companies are simply bad. If you don't believe it, just ask anyone who has ever read a cover letter beginning with, "My enclosed script recently won the quarter finals at the San Antonio screenplay workshop." You will find it truly shocking to encounter so many piles and piles of horrid pages by "writers" so talentless you'd guess that mad cow disease has taken hold of everyone with a laptop in the San Fernando Valley.

This phenomenon (best evoked by the sentence "My mother's dentist wrote a screenplay, would you mind if he sent it to you?") is quite unfair to seriously good writers who study their craft, regardless of what they sell. As you will no doubt quickly learn, the naïveté and arrogance of these weekend scribes is further amplified when you spend your few free hours perusing their medical-thriller-set-on-the-space-shuttle drivel.

Imagine the man-hours and forests that could be saved if only there were some kind of minimum talent requirement for buying screenwriting software. So do we feel guilty encouraging you to skim pages or find preexisting coverage on scripts from your pal, an assistant at an agency? Not in the least. Remember Cliffs Notes in high school? Well, guess what. The world hasn't changed that much.

WRITING COVERAGE: CUT TO THE CHASE

As an assistant working for an agency, production company, or studio, you will inevitably be saddled with weekend script reading. For the most part, your boss will not just ask you what you thought of the script and let you explain in spoken word. He will ask that you write "coverage," a three- to four-page summary of the script.

There is a time-honored formula to writing coverage that really should not be challenged: Begin with a log line, follow it with a two-page synopsis, then write a page of comments, and end with a rating of the characters, dialogue, structure, and plot-line. It is important that you learn how to write good coverage for two reasons. First, and most important, you want to impress your boss. Second, you want to learn how to clearly and eloquently express your ideas about scripts, because in Hollywood everything begins with a script. This is great rehearsal time. A time for you to learn how to critique material, a skill you must develop if you want to succeed.

One screenwriter recalls his first experience in Hollywood thus:

I had a friend in Hollywood, whom I wanted to visit. She was working as an assistant to this crazy guy who would literally hit her over the head with *Variety* when she screwed up. So she quit and started writing coverage. It was a freelance gig for an agency. I think she made about fifty dollars per script. She lucked out, because she got to work at home. So she called me and offered to pay for my ticket if, in exchange, I would write coverage on five scripts at fifty dollars per, earning me two hundred fifty dollars so I could pay her back. She explained to me, "Make it simple, simple, simple. Be an idiot about it, just write clearly. Don't be fancy. Forget that you are a writer. Just write like an elementary school paper, not a college paper. Not deep, Okay? Simple." Despite this advice, it took me the whole week to read the scripts and figure out how to describe them. Mainly because they were just awful scripts, with plots that were so stupid I kept losing track. I spent my entire "vacation" writing coverage. I don't think I ever got a handle on it. But I certainly learned that there are a lot of mediocre scripts in Hollywood. Which encouraged me to write one of my own, which I did, and I sold it.

Lesson: There is no shortage of mediocre scripts in Hollywood and reading them can be inspiration to write a better one of your own. On top of that, it will take a little while for you to become familiar with writing coverage. In the beginning you will labor over every sentence. And consider banal story lines like you actually care. You might even take notes to remember key moments. But after about ten lame scripts you'll be whipping through them, churning out formulaic takes on what are, most likely, already formulaic takes. In general, it is better to keep reading without pausing. You need to get the whole throw of a story in one sitting. If you want to make it easy on yourself, just concentrate on the main character. On their hurdles and payoffs. Then base your general analysis on that.

You start with a log line. This is the first thing your boss will read, so be concise. Every movie has to be summed up in one sentence or no studio will go for it. There has to be a graspable concept, a clear conflict. For example, here is the log line of *Austin Powers: International Man of Mystery* from one piece of coverage: "A swinging, sexually promiscuous secret agent from the mod 1960s is put in cryogenic sleep for twenty years and reawakened in 1997 to stop his arch-enemy. He must cope with the very different present."

A badly written log line rambles from the protagonist's primary conflict and resolution to include too many plot points. A bad version of a log line for *Austin Powers* would be: "A swinging, sexually promiscuous secret agent from the 1960s has this enemy who he used to battle, but then he froze himself, when his enemy froze himself, but then he reawakens, when his enemy wants to take over the world . . ." You get the idea, keep it tight. Think movie posters. Think about those awful movie previews: "This summer, pack your bags and join Shelley Long in a family comedy you'll never forget!" with the inevitable James Brown squeal, "I feel good! *Na na na na na na . . .*"

If the script is disorganized and story lines don't add up or pay off, it will be hard for you to sum it up in one sentence. If this is the case, try your best to write a good log line and then explain in the "comments" section specifically how the movie digresses.

The synopsis should describe what the film is about in two pages. Basically, give about one paragraph for each major turn in the story. The setup is important, make sure your reader knows who the players are as they are revealed. Capitalizing is a helpful indicator. For example, "MARVIN returns from the hospital to find a letter from his wife, LORI, saying that she has run off with another man." Leave out extraneous details and do not editorialize. Tell the story in the order in which the screenwriter tells it. Producers need to be able to see the story for what it is, even if you think it's awful. You never know, a producer may latch on to some nugget of gold in the plot and transform it into a good movie, so don't be sarcastic or condescending in your writing of coverage.

When it comes time to write the comments, you get to express your brilliant opinions about the script. You get to tell the producer or studio or agent whether or not you think the script will sell. It's the great irony of coverage that the people least qualified to do so are getting paid to judge scripts, because those who are qualified are too busy. Be careful with commentary, however, and remember that you are judging a script for its content and commercial potential. Remember also that you are writing about a piece of material that is never finished, so be specific about which parts flake apart and which hold together. Because, chances are, some lucky hack will be brought on to rewrite it. A script might be "well written, funny, and engaging" but "there is no concept holding it together." Or the reverse: "It's a terribly written great story."

Keep in mind for whom you are writing coverage. Studios just want to know if the script can be a big hit. Therefore, you ask yourself: Is it a star vehicle? Will a Richard Gere or a Julia Roberts take the role? Agencies are looking for material for their clients, so you need to think about what directors, writers, and actors might find intriguing about the material. Producers are looking for a script that their company can sell to a studio, so the material needs to match the strengths of the production company. For example, if you are writing coverage for Adam Sandler's production company and you read a traditional adaptation of *Wuthering Heights,* you might want to add in the comment segment that "this material is not appropriate for consideration by a broad comedic actor."

After considering for whom you are reading, think about the genre the movie wants to be. If the script is intended as comedy, treat it as such. Did you laugh? Were the situations amusing? Clever? Original? If it's a mystery, ask yourself: Are the clues planted skillfully? Do the stories intertwine gracefully? Is the process of story revelation captivating until the end? Sometimes you may come across material intended as one thing, though it may be better suited as another. For example, a script written to be a feature may fail because its structure is episodic. However, if the characters and situations are well conceived, it might succeed if developed as a television series.

The following is actual coverage. It was written by an assistant at a major agency, about an early draft of a script that you are most likely familiar with, the massive critical and commercial hit *American Beauty:*

CONCEPT: A kid sits on death row for shooting the father of his girlfriend. Flashback: The father breaks out of a life of quiet desperation, awakening, even as the kid next door romances his daughter, to escape his hell of life. In the end, the wife of the man—not the kid—kills the father, and the innocent kid is sentenced to death.

SUMMARY: RICKY is locked up. His father, THE COLONEL, confronts a detective, FLEISHMAN, with a tape of his son talking to a teenager JANE about hiring him to kill her father, LESTER. ONE YEAR AGO: Lester lives in the suburbs.

His marriage to CAROLYN is cold. There's no sex, no passion, no love between them. She is consumed with her real estate job and making more money. Jane is obsessed with how uncool her parents are and hangs out with the beautiful, nubile ANGELA, a teenage cheerleader/model wannabe. Lester sees Angela cheerlead before a school sporting event and fixates on her powerful sexuality. Jane notices Lester ogling Angela after the event and is creeped out. Angela loves the attention.

Ricky and his militaristic father the Colonel, move in next door. Jane catches Ricky videotaping her from his window, she's annoyed. Ricky approaches Lester and asks him if he wants to get high—the two smoke a joint. Ricky is nineteen, but still in high school. Jane hears rumors about his mental stability. The Colonel collects urine samples from Ricky to make sure he's drug-free, but Ricky just buys clean ones from a nurse, which he substitutes for his own.

Lester hears Angela comment to Jane that she would have sex with her father if he were in better shape. He starts a major work out, health kick. Carolyn is disturbed by his change, she confronts him about their dead marriage. Lester is cocky. She says she won't divorce him because it would hurt her career. Carolyn bites her tongue . . .

Ricky begins to deal pot to Lester. Lester gets fired at work because of "cut-backs," he blackmails the company for a year's worth of salary, and threatens to expose his boss's dirty secrets. He leaves and gets a job at Smiles, a fast-food joint. He doesn't care anymore.

Meanwhile, Carolyn meets LEONARD, a successful and charismatic real estate man. She is enamored with him, he's her hero, they have wild sex.

Ricky is busy videotaping dead pigeons and other ugly objects, and explains to Jane their inner beauty. She's intrigued by his depth, and goes over to his house. He shows her a Nazi war artifact his father keeps. At dinner Carolyn and Lester get into a fight that embarrasses Jane. Later, Ricky videotapes Jane undressing, the Colonel finds him, and beats him severely. Jane sees it all through the window and feels sorry for Ricky, who she now clearly likes. . . . The Colonel remembers satisfying homosexual sex he had in Vietnam. Lester trades in his Camry for a GTO. ONE MONTH LATER: Lester's working out has made a big improvement in his body. His goading of Carolyn is really getting to her. She's euphoric about her affair with Leonard though. Ricky videotapes Jane, often nude, and she loves it. They playfully talk about killing Lester, on tape, but it's a joke. Working the counter at Smiles, Lester sees Carolyn and Leonard come in. He confronts them, riling Carolyn up. Leonard dumps her because he does not want bad publicity due to his divorce. The Colonel, meanwhile, sees a drug exchange between Ricky and Lester but mistakes it for a homosexual meeting; he thinks they are gay lovers. Ricky comes home, Lester fights with him and kicks him out. Ricky takes the $40,000 he has from dealing dope and gets Jane to run away with him.

Angela, hurt, looks for comfort in Lester's now buff arms. He has sex with her. It's her first time. Carolyn, irate, arrives home and blows him away.

THE PRESENT: A whirlwind trial convicts the drug-dealing, mentally challenged Ricky, putting him on death row. Carolyn marries Leonard and they become the King and Queen of Real Estate. . . .

COMMENTS: An edgy, subversive, well-characterized look at the underbelly of American suburban life. *American Beauty* is well worth our attention. The script follows the midlife crisis of Lester, who one day awakens to realize he hates his job, his dependence on his income-earning and cold-hearted wife, and his scornful child. As other forces swirl around him—an oddball teenager next door who romances his daughter, and the resulting alienation of her best friend—he "snaps," quits his job, and has sex with his daughter's friend. His wife, who cares more about success and status than the family, ends up killing him, but the blame is pinned on the weird kid next door.

The script strikes a resounding chord, exposing the roaches beneath the whitewash exterior of the suburbs. The script has a tabloid central concept like Joey Buttafuoco, or Lorena Bobbitt, but examines this "dysfunctional" aspect of family life with intelligence and nuance. This is not *Jerry Springer* stuff, it's a relatively quiet portrait of the bizarre lives of quiet desperation these essentially American characters lead.

Characterization is razor-sharp, totally top-notch, as all members of the central cast grow and become arresting in their own way. Tone is a hallmark, creating a brooding and at times discomforting exposure of the dark side of suburban life. Act One sets Ricky up as the estranged teenage killer, but as the story wears on, we see that his father beats him and that he's actually a bright kid trying hard to survive, who's found an alternative viewpoint. When he gets sentenced to death for a murder he did not do, we feel for him, it's a tragic, dark ending. Same is true for Lester, who tries to awaken himself from the doldrums of a passive, corporate, loveless life. But even this "hero" makes an error, taking the virginity away from a jaded teenage girl and gets killed. Carolyn is a dark, funny character, in spite of herself. It's easy to rave about each character here because they're so well-drawn, and each one turns our expectations on its head and undermines our presumptions. Dialogue is top-notch too, and the delivery is intellectual without being overblown.

Plotting is well-orchestrated and well-managed, creating a character-driven story line that also moves along at a good clip. We become engrossed, involved, and want to turn the page. . . . Suffice to say, the writing is sophisticated well beyond the ways that a log line and comments can sum it up. Satisfying writing. A small scope makes this script possible on a smaller budget—the material lacks megaplex-pleasing commercial edge mainly because it bites the hand of the audience that feeds it. But that's okay; like *The Player*, or other sharp, smart scripts with a subversive eye, this is a story that will find an audience with the art house crowd and viewers dissatisfied with typical fare. A recommend for directors, who will be able to really sink their teeth into the environment, the tone, the characters, and everything else, as there's room here for a visual sensibility and a deft auteur touch. Great stuff.

Characters: EXCELLENT
Dialogue: EXCELLENT
Story Structure: GOOD TO EXCELLENT
Plotline: GOOD

RECOMMEND

Little did this coverage writer know that *American Beauty* would make over $200 million when he suggested, "the material lacks megaplex-pleasing commercial edge." Clearly this assistant knew this was a good movie. You can see it in his comments. But he also says it's only going to fly with an art house crowd. Was he wrong? Not necessarily. The very things he suggested were problematic to a mainstream crowd (the impending death sentence for the boy next door and Lester's taking the young girl's virginity) were rewritten and changed for the film.

Just about everyone in town passed on *American Beauty* before DreamWorks picked it up. When Geffen, Spielberg, Katzenberg, Spacey, and Bening signed on, folks started to feel a little stupid. Then the movie swept the box office and received major critical acclaim and suddenly everyone's looking at their feet thinking, I knew that was a good script, why did I pass again?

Aside from the forgivable mistake of thinking a character-based, dark portrait of suburban life would not please the masses, this is well-written, competent coverage. The writer clearly had a hard time with the log line because *American Beauty* does not hinge on a high concept and involves multiple story lines. The synopsis and comments, however, do justice to the subtlety and depth of the script.

A final note: As a coverage writer, you may feel responsible for whether or not a script gets noticed, and feel some inflated sense of your role in the process of moviemaking. You may think that you might be the lucky schmuck who is thrown the next *Saving Private Ryan*. That you will be able to go to the head of the company and say "this is a great movie" and then become famous for recognizing it. Forget that idea immediately. Assistants are only given the scripts that producers or development girls don't want to read themselves. The higher-ups go through their daily stack of reading and choose the best material for themselves. The crap that has either been around forever and some poor agent continues to hock, or is simply not the kind of material they would ever develop, goes to the assistant.

Second, and more important, just because you wrote the coverage on a script does not mean you discovered it.

When Pigs Fly:
The Art of Hollywood Travel

Hollywood is a trip through a sewer in a glass-bottomed boat.
—Wilson Mizner

FADE IN:

INTERIOR—AMERICAN AIRLINES FIRST-CLASS
CABIN—DAY

FLIGHT ATTENDANT'S POV of a woman covered entirely by a blanket, head to toe. She's been this way for five hours on the flight from New York to L.A. The attendant checks the seating chart. Oh, it's Jennifer Lopez. Across the aisle, two of Hollywood's hottest young stars coo and cuddle, relieved to have found, in a sock, the wad of cash and brick of hash they thought they had lost. In the front row, one of the rapidly rising young British starlets complains that her desired meal is not available. Well, at least it's better than that flight where Connie Stevens had to be restrained and dragged off the plane by police. Sadly, all of the above actually occurred. Though, fortunately, not on the same flight.

An inevitable and important part of the job of an assistant in the entertainment industry is arranging travel. As TV and film production increasingly expands around the country and around

the globe, most executives, agents, and artists must travel extensively, in style, and often at a moment's notice. Big deal, you say
to yourself, I'll just find a good travel agent to call whenever I
need to book anything. Well, you would be sadly mistaken in this
line of thought.

Yes, there are many dedicated travel agents who will be happy to
go through the tedium of checking all flights, fares, hotel, and car
services for you, but the luxury of having an assistant is that the
assistant can "double-check" everything the travel agent finds out.

It may seem to be a waste of time, but you know what? Your
boss doesn't care if half of American Airlines, four travel agents,
and you, the assistant, are all confirming the same facts at the
same time. More than anything, this business of travel is all about
comparison shopping and you get to be the genius who can
instantly multiply mileage by dollars by per diems by time. It's
physics, economics, and freedom of choice. Planning a business
trip becomes a hellish word problem that involves not only creative thinking but the ability to translate, to your boss, vast intri-
cacies, from fare regulations to climate conditions to consulates
and exchange rates.

It's not just as simple as a toll-free line to United. Your boss
realizes that he or she is now able to get someone to do exactly
the kind of travel planning that he or she would never have the
energy to do themselves. What you previously thought was a simple round-trip, domestic flight becomes a "nonstop, midmorning
flight, left aisle of the plane [seat 3B], a carry-on Pekingese, a
Zone-friendly, kosher meal, a curbside meet 'n' greet, and no
check-in required." How about a vacation for your boss and his
eight closest pals, who are invariably Hollywood prima donnas
equally fussy and annoying, and who all want to go to Cuba for
cigars and hookers and fishing. Never mind the federal law pro-
hibiting travel to Cuba at the time you book. Get them there!
One producer's assistant had the wherewithal to obtain fake visas
through London and sneak his boss into Havana via a charter
flight from Nassau. His reward? The boss's screaming phone call

from the Havana airport demanding why he was not told that bribes are standard at Cuban customs and he should've been told to put money inside his passport to avoid its being stamped.

If you've ever looked at a tired, overly manicured airline "representative" methodically clicking away at her computer keys and thought, "Thank god I don't have such a mind-numbing job," look in the mirror, because you will feel a certain affinity with "Debbie" in the not-so-distant future.

The quality of airline sales representatives varies from airline to airline. It's unlikely that you will ever deal with shoddy, flash-in-the-pan airlines—the ValuJets of the world. Instead, you will be dealing with competitive airlines who want to keep the customer happy and are trained to be ridiculously accommodating on the phone. Still, at the end of the day, they are only able to plug in one piece of information at a time, so it is your job to ask them every conceivable combination of dates, mileage awards, certificates, upgrade stickers, routes, and find out about travel restrictions, special weekend fares, vacation offers, and any current discounts.

This can be mutually annoying and unbelievably time-consuming. It's like cross-examining a suspect: "Okay, one more time, you said that the *only* flight available is . . . You're absolutely sure there is *no* other conceivable way to get to . . ." Don't feel too bad about the ticketer on the other end of the line. In fact, the real trick is to make the reservation process fun. Crack jokes. Complain. Why not? They're most likely trapped under tube lighting, clamped to their headsets in some exciting metropolis like Fort Worth. The nicer you are, the more work you'll squeeze out of them (a principle you'll wish your boss would apply). They might even throw in a complimentary upgrade for your efforts. Schmooze the little people. They are your only hope. Not to mention, you are one of them.

One assistant to a producer, because of the producer's pathological fear of flying and his demanding bicoastal occupation, always made it a point to get in good with the travel agent. The assistant always left funny messages and made sure to liven up what could possibly have been the world's most boring conversations with hysterical stories about working for a control freak. Not only did this make life easier on the two of them, but a year later, when the assistant had to plan her own honeymoon on a limited budget, the travel agent stepped up with free upgrade stickers and discounted plane fares. She even called in favors to her friends in hotel management, who gave the newlyweds a master suite in a Parisian hotel at half the price.

THE ONE NUMBER NO ASSISTANT CAN LIVE WITHOUT

Memorize your boss's frequent flyer number immediately. This number means saved money and "upgrades" (the magic word of travel in an industry allergic to coach). If your boss doesn't already accumulate miles through his credit card purchases of endless business lunches and dinners (and we honestly can't imagine who this thriftless loser is), then get him hooked up to an account. It's for your own good.

Naturally, there is the obvious reason that one gets miles from purchases and then can fly for free. But if you do the math in the Hollywood economy of excess and expense accounts, you'll find that there are ways for your boss to seem to spend lots and lots of money that translates into lots and lots of miles. His trip to Maui could end up costing him only what he tips the dude who quietly sends Heidi Fleiss's girls up and down the service elevator.

If your boss uses his frequent flyer credit card for meals for which he is then reimbursed by his company, he walks away from lunch with Kevin Costner at Cipriani's with about 350 miles. If you do some research into the ever-expanding world of miles-for-services, you will find many other reimbursable purchases that contribute to his account: florists, restaurants, long-distance phone calls, cellular phone accounts, rental cars, hotels . . . these are the obvious ones. But read the fine print and you'll find that he can mortgage his house for miles or have his dry cleaning picked up and delivered to earn miles. This is such a rapidly expanding business that by the time this book is published we fully expect illegal immigrant nannies to have tie-in arrangements with major airlines.

You think we're exaggerating here? It is not uncommon for Hollywood players to earn mileage for prostitution services billed "discreetly" to their credit cards. Take the true story of a multimedia magnate whose assistant committed a grave error from which we can all learn. The magnate's sister called the assistant one day and asked for some party-planning help. She wanted to know who Mr. Big Shot used to cater his parties. The assistant didn't know for sure but she did remember seeing lots of charges for "Xanadu Catering" on his airline credit card statements. Great, thanks, 'bye. Imagine sis's shock as she calls "Xanadu Catering" and is asked which specific sex acts she'd like her "caterer" to perform.

All this, of course, is only applicable to travel you must plan yourself. If there is any possible way that a studio will pick up the tab for your boss's trip, well then, even better for you. They'll take care of everything and you won't have to worry about a thing. Studio travel departments are notoriously wasteful. This is a wasteful industry. The studio travel folk know this—do not let them intimidate you, they are used to the excessive demands of star clients. Try for all you can. Specific hotels, car services, car types: "Not a limo, not a cab, a sedan with a phone, the trade papers, and sparkling water." It's perfectly reasonable to ask for a specific airline for mileage purposes. See how far you can go. He has to travel with his wife. She must be able to bring her cocker spaniel. He needs a suite with two very separate rooms as he'll be conducting business. Oh, did you mention the fax, the DVD player, the hypoallergenic pillows, the candles, and—in the case of one network owner—a pack of cigarettes opened, on the table next to the bed, with two cigarettes pulled slightly out.

Bucking for a raise or promotion? Think ahead. Use FedEx. Use the concierge. Have a bath drawn and that night's reading on the bedside table, a bottle of wine, and a medium-rare burger on the way when your boss arrives at the Four Seasons. You can show him or her how meticulous you are on the studio's dime.

FINDING THE MIKE OVITZ OF TRAVEL AGENTS

You want a patient travel agent with a sense of humor. You are going to be working with this person a lot. And you are both going to plan entire international vacations that will be whimsically scrapped when your boss has a "flash of genius" while reading the travel section of the *Times* one Sunday. You are better off with a travel agent who works for fancy Hollywood types and has the up-to-the-minute dish on all the latest spas, resorts, and adventure vacations. And your boss (pack-following, status-starved industry lamb that he is) will probably be comforted to hear the words "Jennifer and Brad were there over Thanksgiving and had a blast." You also want someone who has relationships that can be helpful with the kinds of travel arrangements you'll be making for business trips. An experienced industry travel agent, for example, will know everything about extended accommodation in Toronto, Vancouver, Texas, and North Carolina (popular locations for production these day). These are the people who can take care of you even if the hotel is "booked solid." These hardened professionals know how to make it happen when everything is "sold out." Lucky for you, since your boss will most likely refuse to hear any variation of "all booked": "Just make room at the inn, okay, and don't bother me with the details."

For example, one producer's former assistant (now living under a pseudonym in New Jersey) saved his own job one Friday as the producer headed to Las Vegas, blissfully unaware that his assistant had made reservations for the wrong weekend. In a panic, the assistant called various hotels and found them all completely booked. Fortunately, the assistant thought fast and called the assistant to one of the top agents at William Morris. His boss, he remembered, was old friends with Peter Morton, owner of the

Hard Rock franchise. Fate smiled that day, and by the time the producer arrived, he had stellar accommodations awaiting him, allowing him to gamble away thousands of dollars in style.

A former assistant of Bill's provides the perfect example of when you can push your work on to someone else. In late November, while hiking in the Santa Monica Mountains, Bill ran into his much more successful friend Darren Starr (creator of *Melrose Place* and *Sex and the City*). Darren invited Bill to join him on his Christmas excursion to Africa, a logistical nightmare involving crossing the entire Sahara desert between Morocco and Algeria, which Bill, in turn, dumped on his assistant to figure out. The assistant made the fundamentally wise decision to call Darren's office, figure out who his travel agent is, call her, and basically says, to paraphrase *When Harry Met Sally*, "We'll have what he's having."

The above really illustrates one version of a formula for an assistant with a travel problem. Start with the travel agent. See if they can pull any strings. The second place to go is your imagination. It's time to craft a wonderful story, loosely linked to your boss's reality, that will make any hotelier drool at the chance to you have your cranky, fake-tanned Hollywood boss stay in his establishment. Be careful though, don't overdo it. You don't want your boss to show up at a virtual press conference regarding his "location scout for the next Jim Carrey film."

Drop names and drop them in the context of extreme urgency, all the while explaining that this hotel is a favorite of your boss— make the suckers on the other end of the phone feel good about bending the rules. However, offering bribes is usually a bad idea. First of all, you do not want to be stuck with the phone call from your boss when he arrives, yelling, "I'm not forking out money because you couldn't make it happen!" Additionally, bribery is probably not something with which you want to associate your boss. So, unless your boss specifically instructs you to pass cash under the desk, don't.

Having said that, however, there is a very important distinction to be made between bribery and "generously tipping." In the gratuity department, many first-class service providers are used to obscene overtipping by high-status, service-seeking Hollywood types. There is absolutely nothing wrong with your boss handing the bellboy a hundred if he is expected to run out to the all-night pharmacy to refill a Viagra prescription.

The line begins to blur, though, when you consider the true story of the major movie producer who, staying at a posh NYC hotel, offered the in-house trainer/masseur a thousand dollars for what you might call a "massage with full release." Unbeknownst to the heavyweight producer, the masseur was so insulted by this proposition, he felt free to repeat the encounter to others, including an assistant working on the producer's movie and staying in the same hotel. Within hours, most of the cast and crew had heard about the sleazy event.

The real lesson here is to be extra careful on location. Gossip spreads like wildfire. And speaking of fire, be prepared to deal with stars like the Oscar-winning lead actress in the above-mentioned producer's film. Terribly phobic of fire, hotel fires in particular, she insists that her assistant book her hotel rooms only below the twelfth floor. Why the twelfth, you ask? Because, the starlet learned, most fire truck ladders only reach twelve stories high. Now, while this may sound like an easy request, keep in mind how many hotels have shops and restaurants on their ground floors. Then remember how hotels try to afford special guests some sort of view and above-street-level safety. Suites are generally on the top floors. Put this together and you have the reason why her assistant left for law school.

But that star has nothing on an Academy Award nominee who, finding herself in a suite at the Beverly Hills Four Seasons pressed for time before some premiere or another, called down for a razor to be sent up. Well, we pity the fool who showed up a full twenty minutes later to find the semiclad actress looking like she was about to kill someone.

And what about assistants to stars who are afraid to fly? And there are many of them. They must fend off some of the most illogical and logistically impossible requests from their employers. For instance, one major star will only fly on Boeing 767 aircraft. Why, you ask, already planning another career path? Because the star, after extensive research, concluded that the percentage of accidents per type of commercial aircraft is the lowest on this particular plane. Only problem is, these planes don't fly most routes. Hence, the star spends a lot of time on trains and in Winnebagos.

In fact, to take a different star, Whoopi Goldberg travels almost exclusively in a bus. She, too, is afraid of flying, so she's got an enormous tour bus that she has decorated like a major hotel suite, complete with the finest art and towels. While comfortable for Whoopi, this can occasionally present problems for others. While shooting a recent film at a dangerous location, the producer asked Ms. Goldberg if she would, for security reasons, stay in a nearby hotel. Whoopi responded with something along the lines of "Do they have the towels that I like? Do they have the sheets that I like? Do they have the toilet paper I like? No! You know why? 'Cause it's all in my bus!"

But life can be made easier for the assistant with the queasy boss. It's called "get the studio jet." Phobic flyers will make anyone planning their travel miserable. So why not argue them down? Tell them about the amazing safety record of the privately owned Gulfstream jets. Almost every studio owns at least one. One of the latest Gulfstreams, the G-4, is so smooth and powerful and can fly so high that even Bill's dog, a very phobic flyer brought aboard the Paramount jet, slept on the floor of the cockpit the entire transcontinental flight. So did the usually terrified Diane Keaton, though fellow passenger Goldie Hawn comforted her on takeoff with, "Don't worry, my psychic told me I would never die in a plane crash."

However, not all G-4s are created equal. Bill learned this the hard way en route from Texas to L.A. aboard the Miramax jet, with fellow passenger Leo DiCaprio. It seems that the man to whom the plane belonged, Harvey Weinstein, is fond of lighting up a few cigarettes on board. This led the star of one of his movies to hide herself in the lavatory during most of one flight, trying to breathe oxygen and escape "the flying ashtray" sensation. But it was clearly a preferable situation to what happened when Mr. Weinstein's nicotine craving got the best of him on a Concorde flight from London to New York. It seems that the industry's most colorful mogul ended up arrested for disabling a smoke detector and lighting up in the lavatory. The moral of this story, of course, is not at all that you should obey mundane FAA regulations. No, it's that if you work for a smoker, do yourself a favor and get the private jet. Make an agent call the studio head. Make a lawyer or the star himself call. And if you still have any doubts about the advantages of the G-4, we suggest you compare notes with Mel Gibson's assistant, whose boss had his appendix explode on a commercial flight. There are some things even a Bloody Mary and a warm blanket can't take care of.

But don't think your life's a bowl of warm nuts once you've secured the private jet. Even those stars who own a personal plane, like Bruce and Demi, can make assistants' lives hell. Whenever the couple formerly known as the Willises would travel with their family aboard their jet, they would engage in the endearing ritual of sending their assistant to the trendy L.A. eatery the Ivy, just minutes before their plane was scheduled to take off. The assistant would pick up the predetermined order of grilled vegetable salads and corn chowder and the crucial Ivy bread, which would have to be triple wrapped in foil so that it could arrive at the tarmac *still hot*. Who says airplane food has to be bad?

VACATION: WHY IT'S NO FANTASY ISLAND

A boss's vacation can actually be an assistant's most stressful time. A boss will blame the assistant for any screwups in his quality time with the family he cheats on and neglects the rest of the year. One exec went ballistic when stranded at a Bahamian ferry port, because (shockingly) the boats were not adhering to the published schedule reflected on the assistant's itinerary. In these situations, anger is guaranteed to quadruple.

One successful young screenwriter almost had a seizure when her assistant failed to get her passport to her in time for an international flight. Not that this was entirely the assistant's fault. The screenwriter had forgotten the passport on her journey from L.A. to New York and called the assistant with just a day to spare before boarding a flight to the British Virgin Islands. The dutiful assistant found the passport at the writer's disaster area of a home, had it messengered to the airport, and flown via courier pouch to JFK airport baggage services. Unfortunately, the passport never arrived and the screenwriter was forced to throw herself on the mercy of customs agents on the island of Tortola, hoping they would understand her need for a tan.

But even among these dark nightmares, there are inspiring stories of assistants who stand up in the face of travel adversity. One superagent threw a huge temper tantrum upon arriving at JFK airport with his family to begin their vacation in the Hamptons. The cause? No meet 'n' greet service to help them get their bags into the limo. The assistant gets the call from the enraged agent, now ensconced in his limo en route to Long Island. "I want your resignation in writing within five minutes or I'm calling security to escort you from the building." When the agent called back in five minutes with, "Well, what's your decision? The easy way or the hard way?" The assistant stood up for himself: "You're not firing me and I'm not quitting. This is ridiculous." The assistant launched into a tirade of his own, only to be cut off by a crackling cell phone in the limo. The call was disconnected and the assistant didn't hear from the agent until the following Monday. "Any new calls?" Back to normal. Not another word was ever uttered about the meet 'n' greet scandal.

The assistant even went one better and exacted his revenge by calling the hotel where the agent was staying. He told the general manager his boss was Austrian royalty and told him to fawn over him as much as possible. Then he would order large room service meals and have them delivered at 3 A.M. And what did the assistant get for this miscreant behavior? Well, he is now a rising talent agent at the same agency. Go figure.

You'll Never Reschedule Lunch in This Town Again

Do, or do not. There is no "try."
—Yoda, *The Empire Strikes Back*

If you take all the actresses from the years 1985 to 1999 and added up their lunch tabs paid for by studio executives and then subtracted the amount of food they had vomited, you would still have enough to fund Michael Bay's new action extravaganza.

In Hollywood, it's possible to have six meals a day, typically: 9 A.M. breakfast meeting at the Four Seasons; 10 A.M. breakfast staff meeting; lunch in Beverly Hills or at the studio commissary; drinks at L'Hermitage; dinner at Indochine. Everyone fantasizes that they will be making business deals over gorgonzola crumbles and endive. If only it were a deal a meal. Most often these are just "touching base" jerkoffs at some studio or agency's expense.

When scheduling meetings, the most important thing for an assistant to ascertain is: Who is the alpha dog? The more powerful the individual, the farther others will travel to meet him. This will dictate who decides time and locale as well.

TO CONFIRM OR NOT TO CONFIRM: THAT IS THE QUESTION

The second most important skill for an assistant to possess has to do with the art of scheduling. As screenwriter Syd Field said: "Ninety percent of writing is rewriting." Well, 90 percent of scheduling is rescheduling. Juggling appointments in your boss's busy life will make you priceless.

As for lunches, the fascist schedule of Hollywood dictates that everyone jump into their fully loaded, leased, black BMWs at 12:45, speed dial the office, roll calls from the car before arriving five minutes late to a meal invariably consisting of seared ahi on a bed of greens, which politely ends with all parties pretending to fight over the check between 2:15 and 2:30.

Once the meeting is set and the day arrives: to confirm or not to confirm. That is the question. Most of the time, your boss will not want to see most of the people on his schedule. Especially lunch meetings. They can be tedious hassles and a vague dance, always including the phrase, "We'd love to be in business with you." This inevitably leads to a game of chicken, where each office will avoid confirming or canceling as long as possible, with the hope that the other will cancel first. In an extreme scenario, neither will call until 12:50 P.M.

SHOULD YOU LIE OR JUST NOT TELL THE TRUTH?

If push comes to shove and you must cancel the meeting, you must decide: Should I lie or just not tell the truth? There is a Clintonian distinction that must be fully understood before you venture into the sticky quicksand of Hollywood excuses. For instance, if your boss chooses to get a massage at lunchtime, it is acceptable to tell his spurned date: "I'm so sorry, he's having trouble with his back and had to go see a specialist." However, it is unacceptable to say, "Sorry, he's sick." And if your boss gets busted, don't think for a second he won't blame it on you. That's why it is mandatory you learn how to avoid lying by learning how to not tell the truth.

HOW VALET PARKING CAN CHANGE YOUR LIFE

Small oversights can come back to haunt you in big ways. One of the most common mistakes revolves around where you may arrange his meals. Did you forget he's allergic to shellfish? Is he on a diet? Does the restaurant have valet parking? Did you confirm the reservation? Does his ex-wife go there often? The importance of picking up the minute details of your boss's life cannot be overstated. A small forethought now can save bad tantrums later.

One assistant nearly got fired for stupidly scheduling a lunch for his boss at the Grill. The assistant had been told time and again, "Anywhere in Beverly Hills but the Grill, the parking is a nightmare." This assistant assumed his boss was being fussy and ridiculous as the Grill is the Hollywood hotshot headquarters between 1 and 2 P.M. Surely, it's worth finding parking to brush elbows with Sherry Lansing.

The assistant finally realized the extent of his mistake when he had the misfortune of having to lunch there himself. It turns out, the Grill (basically an overpriced, glorified Sizzler set amidst a faux-nineteenth-century street plaza in Beverly Hills, just spitting distance from half the agencies) has a nasty grilled chicken salad and an even nastier parking arrangement. The garage is down the street, and after lunch you are forced to wait in line with tourists in a carbon monoxide–filled, underground valet area, with Romanesque pillars separating the BMWs and SUVs. Agents hover at the mouth of the garage in fear of losing service on their cell phones. By the time you get your car, you're sick from the Caesar salad dressing and the car fumes and you have to pay the valet ten bucks just to escape. Lesson learned.

The Domestic Drama: Even Michelle Pfeiffer's Toilet Floods

The people are unreal. The flowers are unreal; they don't smell. The fruit is unreal; it doesn't taste of anything. The whole place is a glaring, gaudy, nightmarish set, built up in the desert.

—Ethel Barrymore

No matter whom an assistant works for in Hollywood, chances are that some form of domestic drama will occur. This does not necessarily mean that assistants end up in the middle of gunplay between spouses, but more likely they will end up putting out fires of a more mundane nature on the homefront.

For example, one star's assistant we talked to would routinely receive breathless phone calls in the middle of the night when the star's alarm system would go off, echoing "intruder alert . . . intruder alert." After racing over in the middle of the night several times, the assistant now knew this was due to the wind blowing open various windows in the star's mansion. But each occurrence still entailed 4 A.M. calls to the alarm company, the police, sometimes even the neighbors. Add to the assistant's job description: security specialist.

The job description for the Hollywood assistant includes many domestic skills that one might not realize will be necessary. Auto mechanic, child psychologist, animal behaviorist, swimming pool technician, landscaping coordinator, home electronics repairman, and computer specialist are just a few. Perhaps you didn't know that many assistants who must deal with domestic responsibilities at a boss's home need to be somewhat fluent in Spanish. How else can you tell the gardener to move the cactus away from the children's tree house or tell the housekeeper to cover the Monet before she dusts the light fixtures? The fact is, most domestic help in Los Angeles is Latin American, so potential Anglo assistants better get with el programo.

It is important to realize that a Hollywood estate, particularly a star's home, is really a factory of sorts. It employs dozens of various workers year-round and the assistant often serves as the foreman of the crew. The assistant will interface with the domestic staff as well as the outside laborers and repairmen. And since most Hollywood homes seem to be undergoing some kind of construction at all times, it is not unusual for an assistant to discuss blueprints, budgets, and security with construction workers and contractors.

Keep in mind that a good assistant has to be willing to live the unglamorous parts of his or her boss's life. Don't feel like getting your car washed? Don't worry, you won't have time to after getting your boss's car washed, detailed, deodorized, and tuned up. Thinking about getting a pet? Why bother, since you'll be taking care of the celebrity dogs during most holidays when you-know-who heads to St. Barths.

Yes, you're living your life vicariously, but think of all the pluses! You'll know everything there is to know about where to find a good nanny or nursery school, having done extensive research for the boss. You'll become an expert on vets and dog walkers and groomers. Many charity groups will appreciate all the time and hard work you've put in so that your boss can take the credit and the tax deduction. And think of all the practice you'll have writing thank-you notes! Did you ever expect you'd get paid to learn forgery?

STARVING FOR DOLLARS: HOLLYWOOD'S EATING DISORDERS

Perhaps the most unexpected education most Hollywood assistants receive comes in the area of celebrity nutrition. Food, it's the basic block of life. It's how us animals keep on keeping on. It's the thing that separates us from the vegetables. It's simple. Without it we're dead. It's our energy that, in most cultures, is consumed at three separate mealtime occasions known as breakfast, lunch, and dinner. You may be familiar with the food pyramid that they teach in elementary school with grains, fruits, and vegetables on the bottom, then meats, then fat at the very top. It's sensible. The school, the state, your mother, they all believed in it, but when you come to Hollywood it all changes.

And it changes all the time. The food pyramid is under constant attack and renovation, not unlike most of the scripts under development at every studio. Carbohydrates at the bottom, carbohydrates at the top, fats take over, meats are eliminated, meats are back, fats are out, fats are in, fats are really in. One assistant reports his agent boss doling out the nutrition advice at a breakfast meeting with a colleague thus: "Dude, fat? Okay, it like slows down the absorption of glucose into the bloodstream, it's good for you." "No way," says the other agent, miserably looking at his egg white omelette. "Way, you need it, it makes you thin," says the other agent, busting a yolk all over his sausage. "Fat provides the building blocks for the body's hormones. It's all true, it's the Zone, dude, haven't you heard?"

The Zone. It's a book, it's a million websites, it's a major diet industry, and it's probably your boss's new religion. "If all bread left the face of the earth, we'd have a much healthier planet," declares the author of the best-selling book, and your boss who's just summoned you to bring him the five o'clock snack. The Zone snack is a sad-looking Tupperware box containing two slices of Swiss cheese, a couple of apple crescents, and a single walnut in what looks like a urine sample cup. Forty-30-30: 40 percent carbs, 30 percent protein, and 30 percent fat.

The Zone. It's big now, though it will probably fade when all the hideous kidney diseases the antifad doctors warn of start cropping up and we're back to spaghetti and bagels again. But right now there's not an actress in Hollywood who'll be caught dead with a noodle on her fork. In the eighties it was aerobics and pasta, pasta, pasta (low fat). Then there were shakes; oh, and there were shakes before, in the seventies, but they were *Rocky* shakes with eggs and soy sauce. The newer ones had amino acids and blue-green algae.

The citizens of Hollywood swore by blue-green algae in the spring of '96. "It's nature's Prozac," they piped, "the coffee of the sea," "You will literally add years to your life!" More years to follow diet trends, spend tons of money, and continue to be roughly the same weight. Then there was the great polyunsaturated/monounsaturated fat debate of '91, the Nayonaise and Not Dog flash-in-the-pan of '89, and the spinach–egg white boom of '95. It's really hard to keep up. It's not just in Hollywood, it's an American thing, but in Hollywood more than any other place in America, almost everyone takes these trends as gospel for a minute or five and then goes on to the next. If you fall behind in the great food pyramid debate of the millennium, you'll find yourself fending off the disapproving, perhaps shocked and disgusted glare of your Hollywood peers when you order the wrong food group.

"Do the pancakes come with the potatoes?" asked one assistant at the trendy Holly Hills Diner, in the summer of '99. Well, the waiter (a struggling actor), the assistant's breakfast date (a D-girl), and the nearby table of junior agents who overheard all dropped their jaws in horror at the vulgar carb eater.

In Southern California, the Zone diet has mushroomed from a lifestyle choice to an industry. "Life Zone," a health club devoted solely to putting people on Zone diets, has seen 1,500 customers in the past two years enlist in its twelve-week program. At the bistro L.A. Farm, a hot spot for film moguls, one-third of lunch orders come from a Zone menu introduced last year.

One assistant to the producer of about ten multimillion-dollar teen flicks actually overheard his boss raging, "You are an idiot, because bread literally decreases your mental acuity!" People get religious about this stuff. It's absurd. They get defensive and talk about glucose and hormones as if they're biologists. They'll say things like, "Well, you just have to calculate your body mass index," casually over a crustless pizza at one of the many restaurants now catering to this trend. If Madonna, Brad Pitt, Bernadette Peters, Matt Dillon, the cast of *Baywatch*, Winona Ryder, and Howard Stern take this seriously so shall you, the assistant.

"Leave Everything to Us—We Do the Work for You" promises one Zone delivery outfit, and this is where the assistant comes in. As an assistant, you are dealing with people who do not even question the notion that they can hire anyone to do anything to make them better, richer, thinner, more spiritual, toned, well-read, stylish, evolved, self-aware . . . you name it. And maybe they can. Maybe an army of employees, each dedicated to the various basic needs of your boss, can help. But maybe you are dealing with a person who cannot dress themselves, know when they are hungry and for what, keep in good physical condition without some overpaid muscled Barney yelling "four more"; a person whose beautiful house was done in a week by Brad Pitt's decorator for a cool million, a person whose spirituality is confirmed by "the" yoga guru to the stars who chants, "Let go of all your baggage" and suddenly a day's worth of suspect and self-serving activity in the workplace is swept from the mind. Guilt free. Fat is good for you, it turns out. Anything can be spun. It's the con.

When you work for fancy Hollywood people, you get to house-sit for fancy Hollywood people. This can be a great opportunity to vicariously live the life of the face-lifted for weeks at a time. But sometimes these house-sitting adventures can be more like *Risky Business.* One assistant was lucky enough to regularly stay in his boss's Malibu mansion where he could enjoy spectacular sunsets, cabinets full of free booze, an endless supply of the kind "bud," nine hundred channels, surround-sound speakers, and sheets of the highest thread count.

Knowing full well that winning over a chick would depend on a lot more than his mediocre looks and dull personality, this assistant decided to take the car—the sports car, the car that he was never supposed to drive—for a drive. And not just any drive, he drove from Malibu all the way along the Pacific Coast Highway, onto the 10, through the endless flats, past the Hollywood Hills, all the way to East L.A. where some kind of Tibetan Freedom Rally was taking place. Once there, he immediately got loaded up on a variety of substances and as he took a drag off his boss's one-hitter, while leaning against the car, he saw the girl of his dreams: a crazy-hot, Fiona-Apple-Bomb, eighteen-year-old punk chick. After he seduced her with the Chivas he had chillin' in the backseat she agreed to come home with him to the Malibu spread. But now he was too plastered to drive the $100,000 car. So she drove, but she didn't have a license. When they got home, they had sex in every room in the mansion, taking full advantage of features like the Jacuzzi, the zebra rug, the island in the kitchen . . . which was all well and good, except he foolishly let his $400 glasses fall on the floor.

While otherwise engaged, our assistant didn't notice the dog mangling the glasses, leaving only the two lenses lying on the floor. Our hero couldn't afford new frames for his glasses, so he crafted a pair out of a black plastic video rental box.

On Monday at work, he looked like a comic book version of legendary agent Swifty Lazar. Everybody asked what happened to his glasses, and he ad-libbed a bicycle accident, counting his blessings that at least the only damage done was to his own belongings. That was until he got back to his temporary Malibu home and found the eighteen-year-old had made off with whatever valuables she could stuff into her knapsack.

Hollywood bosses should be wary of the assistant who is too close in the domestic arena, for it is this proximity that can cause the most damage. Take the case of the major media mogul whose assistant had been fed up with his shabby treatment for quite some time. The mogul asked the assistant to program one of his home VCRs for him. No problem, the assistant did as instructed. But as he was fiddling around with the machine, he found there was a VHS tape inside that contained some truly astonishing footage. Footage of the homemade variety. Footage concerning the mogul and his wife, and another woman, and a feather boa. And some sex toys. In other words . . . the jackpot for this particular, badly treated young man. Did he steal the tape? Of course not. Did he copy it? Naturally.

Soon thereafter, one of the frequent rounds of abuse led, at long last, to the assistant's dismissal. The assistant now sought his revenge, and, as reported in *Salon* magazine, actually sent the explicit sex tape to *Hustler* publisher Larry Flynt. But due to the truly huge stature of the mogul involved, Mr. Flynt called him and they reached a media-mogul-to-media-mogul understanding. The tape was buried. Hence, the world was denied the opportunity to see said mogul screaming in erotic ecstasy while trying out the latest in dildo technology at the hands of his wife.

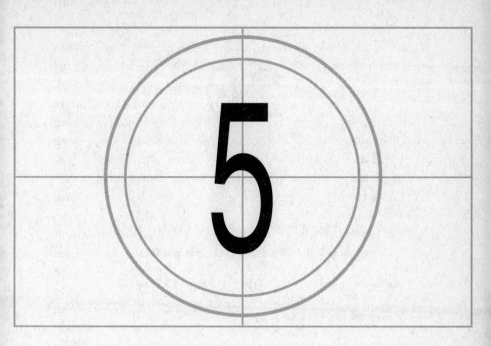

THE WRAP PARTY

Sex, Drugs, and Other Work-Related Issues

Agents used drugs. Clients used drugs. Producers and studio executives and shopaholic wives used drugs.

—Frank Rose, *The Agency*

So, you place the call to the pot delivery service. Maybe you risk FedEx-ing some Quaaludes to the location where your boss is filming. Maybe you even rendezvous with "Mr. Del Mar," the two-hundred-pound coke dealer to the stars. But do you actually cook up some freebase and ignite the rock for your boss if he needs you to? How do you know when to draw the line in the drug-addled world of Hollywood?

Cocaine isn't as openly used as it was in the eighties, but it hasn't gone away. Not by a long shot. In Hollywood there is, and will always be, a floating eighties coke posse. There will be busts and humiliations for stars. There will be powerful and respected studio or agency heads snorting up rope-size, frosty lines with the latest box office sensation. And there will be the young assistants who don't have the rebound capacity of their hardened employers and will find themselves hungover and unemployed in no time.

The Hollywood "community" has a double standard when it

comes to drugs: You can do drugs once you're in power, but as you're climbing the ladder, you had best keep it discreet. Don't get any ideas from some of the big managers and movie legends routinely seen hoovering up Colombia's finest at Saturday night parties and in Beverly Hills Hotel bungalows. There's really nothing more vulgar and pathetic than a coked-out assistant blabbing company gossip indiscriminately to a bunch of dismayed party guests at Cafe Les Deux. So remember, you can party when you're rich and famous, but for now, put the rolled up c-note down and go memorize the latest edition of the Creative Directory.

But to be honest, you might have to do some dirty work. One notorious producer had his assistant score six grams of cocaine for a star-studded birthday party. Another assistant had to roll eighty joints for his boss, the president of a high-powered management company, so he could hand them out at a party he was hosting. One agency assistant was actually flown to South America to pick up a full kilo of cocaine and flew back the same day, only to be arrested at customs. She ratted on her boss, but they both paid a dear price. A geeky, twenty-one-year-old assistant once had to arrange for twelve "high-class" hookers to be flown in from New York for an exclusive agency party. The assistant actually had to attend the party, making sure that various high-profile sleazebags were being "taken care of."

This brings us to the sticky question of sex in Tinsel Town . . .

SLEEPING YOUR WAY TO THE MIDDLE: HOW TO GET AHEAD WITHOUT GIVING HEAD

> *They go to bed with Gilda, they wake up with Rita.*
> —Rita Hayworth

Everyone in Hollywood wants what they can't get. So don't give it up. Tease, tease, tease. Be a *"Rules* girl." Sure, Monica Lewinsky managed to parlay a blow job into a book deal, an agent, millions of dollars, a quality hour with Barbara Walters, immunity, and finally a reason to drop thirty pounds, but we cannot, in good faith, encourage this strategy. Sex is only as good as long as it lasts and the repercussions of dropping to your knees for someone superior to you will reaffirm only one thing: their superiority.

Do not attempt to sleep your way to the top. You may have heard rumors that supermodels have gotten parts for this, but we're betting you're not a supermodel. And a sloppy one-night stand will most likely put an end to a potential business connection. Even if you're a master in the sack, sleeping around is still a no-no. People talk, and if it gets back to your boss that you give a mean blow job, your credibility will be shot.

Of course, dating within the industry is inevitable and it can be very beneficial. Be an opportunist; take the date, if you feel you can benefit from his or her experience in the business (not in the sack). Date all you want. But don't get plastered, do take a separate car, and be home by eleven. We know it sounds harsh, but the deal is you're in boot camp, not booty camp. This is a mean-spirited, ego-driven, gossipy town, not Plato's Retreat.

And by the way, you're too stressed out and overweight from months of sitting on your ass and eating cake at weekly going-away parties for terminated coworkers whose Tom Arnold projects have just bombed to offer much in the way of a fulfilling sex life. Your love story, shall we say, is not even the "C" story line in the movie of your assistant life. Not to mention this picture has been rated "PG-13" by the Motion Picture Association of America.

If you are one of the few that can maintain a healthy sex life with a coworker or someone in the business during these degrading years of servitude, then keep it on the down-low. First of all, no one cares. Second of all, you want to remain as neutral as possible in the eyes of your boss. If he knows you're dating within the biz, the thought will cross his mind that your pillow talk will most likely include unbridled paragraphs of boss-bashing. Dating an assistant, everyone knows, is dating the human repository of all his or her boss's bad energy.

On that note, you better have a strong relationship with some-one if you're going to open your mouth about your boss's private affairs. Remember the assistant discretion pact even when you are exhausted and you want to vent. It's all about the "nondisclosure bitch session." You may find this hard, as the conversations that pass between your boss and his spouse or ex-spouse or lover or hooker can be quite titillating or terrifying, depending on the quality of their psycho-sexual issues.

One assistant to the producer of many successful Disney movies had to endure his boss's regular booty calls to young men. It was his way to pump himself up with testosterone between meetings. Booty call, conference call, booty call, conference call.

A young, attractive, completely inexperienced girl, whom we'll call Sybil, was hired as the assistant to the president of a major studio. Before long they were sleeping together. This went on for a brief stint until she decided that she wanted more out of the "relationship" than he was willing to give. He tried to back off, at which point she slapped him with a sexual harassment suit with the help of a high-profile sexual harassment lawyer. Naturally, he immediately gets her a promotion to the story department in order to shut her up. Of course, she is completely underqualified for this job and everyone in the department is annoyed and con-fused by her presence. Soon she meets a top box office–grossing superstar in a meeting and before long they're sleeping together. When he realizes she's a psycho and he wants her out of his life, he personally calls the president of another studio and gets him to hire her as a VP to get her away from the studio where his film is in development.

At the new studio, coworkers could make neither head nor tale of her bizarre behavior. She would sleep in the office during busi-ness hours and had no sense of boundaries in the workplace. One day she straddled a shocked VP in his office. She wasn't wearing underwear. Finally, she started stalking the president, who had initially hired her. He would do anything to keep her at a dis-tance. But eventually she started to drive by his house and throw scripts over his fence or simply wait to try to catch him coming and going.

Finally, the studio head couldn't take it and stuck her on a movie shooting in Texas just to get her out. Who knows what happened to Sybil, but one thing's for sure: her name is nowhere to be found in the current Creative Directory.

One young assistant-turned-screenwriter really screwed herself when she decided that a summer of fumbling, tequila-laced sex jaunts with a series of New York indie icons would get her recognized on the New York film scene. Think again, honey. Those hungover scenesters have not read a script of hers to date. In fact, one of the actors just got nominated for a Golden Globe, and our girl is currently looking for another assistant job.

But there are people who sleep their way to the middle. One intern who worked for an up-and-coming production company was about to be offered a job as assistant to the president when word got out that she was getting it on with the soon-to-be-fired director of development. The job offer was immediately reconsidered and she became the object of scathing office gossip. A year later, what is she doing? Working as a highly paid assistant to the head of the top management company in Hollywood. What do you know? Who did she blow?

Another assistant happily pulled down her skirt and adjusted her lipstick after a happy hour "quickie" with a power agent in the parking lot of the Wilshire Boulevard agency where they both worked. Little did she know, as she ascended the elevator on the way back to her cubicle, that the parking attendant was already replaying the garage surveillance tape of their not-so-romantic dalliance on the hood of what we can only assume was a black BMW. By the end of the week, the tape had circulated though the offices. Then one day, presumably when the power agent got wind of this, the tape disappeared and the story was squashed (though clearly not completely destroyed). What happened to the girl who just couldn't say no? Now she's a full-fledged agent at that very same agency.

Moral of the story? It all depends on who you blow, how you blow, and why you blow. If it's scot-free of any romantic expectations and you are more concerned with your job at the end of the day, a little insider sex trading can't hurt. Or can it?

Beware the wrath of the jealous girlfriend. Even if you're not hiding the salami, in many ways you are closer to your boss than their own love interest. You know everything and often the spouse relies on you for information.

We know one attractive, smart, and ambitious woman who, when she was an assistant to a major film director, was continually tormented by a jealous girlfriend. This girlfriend was an out-of-work model, one of those smooth-calved, collagen-implanted, frosty-lidded fixtures loitering in front of the Coffee Bean on Sunset Plaza. She would leave voice messages at 4 A.M. (a time apparently conducive to unemployed model career advancement strategizing), demanding that the assistant dig up various tear sheets from obscure French fashion magazines. Said assistant would be on the phone to Paris, stretching the limits of her high school French to obtain the scant evidence that this girl was, in fact, a model. Despite this hard work, the "model" continued to feel threatened by the assistant's closeness to the director, to the point where she actually called the assistant one morning and announced, "You're fired, you have to pack everything up and leave the office before he gets in. He wants you out." Our assistant was panicked and sure that she had done something terribly wrong. She spent a grueling two hours in the office, afraid for her job, only to find out, when her boss finally arrived, that none of this was true and her job was safe. Well, for a while anyway. When the death threats started coming in, our earnest assistant had to quit. The clearly unstable "model" ended up getting pregnant and forcing nuptials. She then became addicted to drugs and was declared clinically insane. The director fought for custody and got the kid. But Hollywood loves a sequel. The model ended up doing the same thing with a studio head and is now married with kids . . . again. Bottom line, stay out of the way of

Hollywood trophy girlfriends and wives; they're fierce, phony, and have way too much time on their hands.

Having said that, here's a tale of true romance about an assistant who got tangled up with his boss's wife and escaped, reputation intact. One hot, summer afternoon he went to his boss's house in the Hollywood Hills to drop something off and then head home. When he arrived, his boss's wife, whom we shall refer to as Mrs. Please-don't-sue-us, asked this young assistant to join her in the pool for a quick dip. He tried to refuse but she kept insisting. The next thing you know they're toweling off and she's suggesting a quick hose down in the steam shower. One thing led to another and this young, excited, and terrified boy was instructed to be creative with the removable shower nozzle. Lucky for him, she never talked.

And another story from the mixed-up files of bad Hollywood marriages: A major television executive had his assistant lie to his wife and family and create fake flight itineraries to London so that he could have an in-town affair. The assistant had to make hotel and rendezvous arrangements with the executive's mistress, as well as send flowers and love "sussies" billed to the assistant's own credit card, so that his wife did not see the "unwanted" expenses on his statements. He also made this assistant wrap all of his Hanukkah gifts for his family and even had her pass off a baby outfit that the girlfriend bought for his nine-month-old son as a gift he chose himself. The same executive sent this assistant on drug runs, often for multiple ounces of pot, and had her FedEx (on the studio's dime) a package of cocaine to the mistress; the assistant had to "eyeball" the value, which was in the high hundreds.

Perhaps even more horrifying is the story of the assistant who had to function as intermediary between his boss and the poor woman he was divorcing. Even the most jaded lawyer would be shocked by the abusive and vindictive messages this assistant had to relay. He would hear the deep sadness and grief in the voice of his boss's wife and then offer up, "He says, 'You're not getting a penny, and you'll be lucky if you see your kids again.'"

Hey, you're just the messenger.

Speaking of which, here's an example of when too much information about your boss's sex life can really get your stomach churning. One producer's assistant had to try very hard to ignore the sight of a young male hooker dashing toward the bathroom as his boss opened the door to his hotel room. Let's just say that there was a very notable substance in his boss's beard that recalled Ben Stiller's famous scene in *There's Something About Mary*.

An assistant's fear of getting fired can be channeled into titillating foreplay. A tyrannical producer once left his young, male assistant to house-sit. One night, this assistant was relaxing with about fourteen or fifteen scripts in his boss's gaudy Brentwood estate, when a sexy blonde (the assistant to the star of his boss's current blockbuster) showed up at the doorstep to drop off a script. He invited her in and the two ended up bonding, as only beleaguered, stressed-out assistants can bond, and the next thing you know, they're rolling around in the master bedroom. "That was the greatest moment, the assistant to the star of his movie. God, what was her name? She had blond hair, she was a lunatic. The panic that he might come home was such a turn on." He can't remember her name, but he'll never forget the thrill of worrying that his boss might suddenly walk in and catch him. Whatever floats your boat.

A perfect example of bizarre Hollywood sex tales took place on the grounds of notorious producer Don Simpson's Bel Air estate. When his assistant showed up at the house one night, for an 11 P.M. meeting, he discovered a distressed young woman tied to a tree. Weeping, she begged him to untie her. When the assistant went inside and told Simpson that the woman was in pain, Simpson angrily replied, "That woman is being paid a lot of money to be tied to that tree!"

Some of the most sordid Hollywood sexcapades were revealed in the book *You'll Never Make Love in This Town Again*, authored by four prostitutes and three ghostwriters. This is mandatory reading for any youngster heading to Hollywood who wants to know the depths of the depravity that fame provides. These are the stories told by the actual women who've slept with Vanna White, urinated on the former head of Paramount, had rough, one-minute sex with Warren Beatty, copulated with John Ritter in a kitchen for nine hours, been pissed on by Jack Nicholson, humiliated by Timothy Hutton, sodomized by Matt Dillon in a sauna, and whipped and beaten by some of the top names in Hollywood.

While some of the more recent stories, like Hugh Grant caught with prostitute Divine Brown on Sunset Boulevard, not far from where cops found Eddie Murphy picking up a transvestite in the middle of the night, have become the fodder for nighttime talk show monologues, the reality of what happens when the famous seduce newcomers can be terrifying and often tragic.

As an assistant, you will need to be prepared for anything these lunatics might get into. It is entirely possible you could be dragged into the unseemly world of celebrity sex scandals. For example, what if you were a big box office star's assistant on the set of a film where he was rumored to have left his mike on after returning to his trailer for some "quality time" with a woman who was taking good care of the star? If the sound crew could hear, over their headsets, the explicit and lewd mutterings as the star gave instructions to his female companion, should his assistant knock on the trailer door and interrupt his famous boss with the info that everyone was all too aware of what was happening? Or would it be better to play dumb?

From Under the Red Carpet: Assistant Life at a Hollywood Premiere

Don't look at me. I was up until 4 A.M. at the goddam premiere of The Bible. *Premieres! I will personally kill that John Huston if he ever drags me into another mess like that. There must have been ten thousand people clawing at me. I get claustrophobia in crowds and I couldn't breathe. Christ, they started off by shoving a TV camera at me and yelling, "Talk, Ava!" At intermission I got lost and couldn't find my goddam seat after the lights went out and I kept telling those girls with bubble hairdos and the flashlights, "I'm with John Huston," and they kept saying, "We don't know no Mr. Huston, is he from Fox?" There I was fumbling around the aisles in the dark and when I finally found my seat somebody was sitting in it, and there was a big scene getting this guy to give me my seat back. . . . On top of it all, I lost my goddam mantilla in the limousine. Hell, it was no souvenir, that mantilla. I'll never find one like it. . . . And after it's all over, what have you got? The biggest headache in town. Nobody cares who the hell was there. Do you think for one minute the fact that Ava Gardner showed up at that circus will sell that picture? Christ, did you see it? . . . Anyway, nobody cares what I wore or what I said. All they want to know anyway is was she drunk and did she stand up straight. This is the last circus. I am not a bitch! I am not temperamental! I am scared, baby. Scared. Can you possibly understand what it's like to feel scared?*

—Ava Gardner talking to Rex Reed after the opening of John Huston's *The Bible*

All Ava is trying to say is that movie premieres are not the fantasy you see on *Entertainment Tonight*. A Hollywood premiere is a meat market. It's a great big glamorous press junket. A festival of promotion to put the movie, the stars, and the designers of the stars' clothes on the map, if only for opening weekend. All that glitters is certainly gold for the E! Network, which is basically the distribution channel for the industry. Premieres are often described as "free advertising" but, essentially, they are very big, very expensive campaigns.

WHAT ARE THEY REALLY THINKING?

At a premiere it's all hugs and laughter. Everyone makes nice-nice. It's like the fighting married couple who pull it together for the dinner party and then start fighting again on the way home. Inevitably, the making of a movie is riddled with anxiety, battles, and resentment. Inevitably, a premiere will reflect another film-making experience altogether. The director will get up in front of the enthused industry audience and talk of a "passionate vision," and that he "couldn't have asked for a more talented cast, a more understanding studio." Meanwhile, what he's thinking is: It's a miracle we made this thing! The studio screwed us, everyone tried to bail out of the movie. We had to sue. . . . No, at the premieres it's all a big lovefest where the people involved at least pretend to forget about the hellish ride that got them there.

In fact, during the making of one of Paramount's most successful films, two of the three stars tried to quit, one had to be threatened with a lawsuit to finish the movie, and the director actually came to blows with the producer. He was even hospitalized during production. But when it came time for the premiere, you can bet it was all hugs and kisses, and "wasn't that wonderful working together."

If the movie makes money everyone will continue this ruse, collaborate in a revisionist history, and start scheming a sequel. If it's a bomb, they have permission to hate one another again. The masks will drop and everyone will be blaming everyone else: "I'm telling you, the studio cut out the core of the story, we were neutered!" Or, "It was marketing, they sold it as something it's not." But for one brief, shining moment, the premiere can be a magical time for those involved, false though it may often be.

The director gets to have the rare and fleeting experience of an ideal industry audience who will clap and yelp with enthusiasm no matter what comes on the screen. The agents, who case the lobby of a premiere like dogs around a dining room table, get a schmooze smorgasbord. The studio executive, who was promoted for bringing this picture in, finally gets some attention. The relatives of various players in the movie get to quake with joy as they rub elbows with Will and Jada at the after-party buffet. Even the limo drivers are happy because half the streets surrounding the movie theater are carefully cordoned off for their convenience. The publicists are busy, this is their bread and butter. The photographers are gleefully focusing their lenses on Julia Roberts's well-flossed teeth. The "journalists" need only extend their microphone and a celebrity speaks. It is a heightened experience for all involved.

However, as Ava pointed out, a premiere can be torture for a star. Granted, she might have been drunk and didn't want her bloodshot eyes to be the subject of tabloid gossip, but she has a point that any star can relate to. It's a fishbowl, baby, and you are contractually obligated to swim for the audience. Almost without exception, a star's contract states that he or she must publicize the movie. They have to get out there and ham it up for the press, it's their job. Do you think that Jennifer Love Hewitt was out there peddling *Can't Hardly Wait* because she thought it would be a huge hit? Think again, it was in the contract.

Most stars are willing to do whatever it takes to make their movie a financial success. A box office bomb is just as bad for a star as it is for a studio. Given this, the timing of each star's stint on the red carpet is crucial. Celebrities need to have adequate time to talk small with the press. They cannot be bumping into one another, they need their own spotlight. This means that there is a PA and an assistant in constant communication with the red carpet and the limousines, making sure arrivals are synchronized.

AN ASSISTANT'S ROLE: NO FREE POPCORN FOR YOU

As an assistant, you could have varying feelings about premieres, but you will definitely be affected by their influence in some way. If you work for a star, you'll be dealing with their clothes, tickets, transportation to and from the premiere, related publicity, appearances, accommodations, and interviews. If you work for the producer of the premiering movie, you will be working hand in hand with the studio publicity team to make sure everything is taken care of, from the RSVP list, to seating arrangements, to the theme of the after party, to the flower arrangements, to the parking. If you work for the studio, you will be placing the calls between the executive on the project and the publicity team. Mostly, you will be dealing with people calling for tickets and you will make sure all the important people are taken care of. If you work for the director, you will be trying to get more tickets from the studio for the many friends and relatives your boss must have in attendance. As an assistant to the publicity studio folks, you're up to your neck in every aspect of making a premiere happen. You'll be there with a headset frantically multitasking. Everything is on your shoulders. The stakes are high, it's a huge logistical nightmare: premieres are always overbooked, behind schedule, and there is inevitably some mix-up resulting in Spike Lee and Spike Jonze having been assigned the same seat. You will learn that a premiere is just a little bit like making a movie, but you only get one shot.

Following that logic, if you can throw a smooth premiere, you've got what it takes to produce. As an assistant, use these occasions to prove your coordinating skills and you'll be noticed. Moving the masses is what much of moviemaking comes down to. Seating guests is like positioning the extras for a big set piece, and once the projector starts rolling, all you can do is sit back and pray.

THE AFTER PARTY

Up to half a million dollars is often spent on the after party alone. The parties become like movies themselves, with elaborate sets built around the theme of the movie. For Tom Hanks's *That Thing You Do*, a parking lot in the middle of Century City was transformed into a "state fair," with grazing cows, pigs, and a Ferris wheel. Guests to the *Boogie Nights* party got to pose on a huge bed with fake porn stars as a disco cover band cranked out perfect renditions of "Boogie Fever," "Boogie Shoes," and "Boogie Wonderland." The *Lethal Weapon 4* party had an Asian theme and guests were bussed from Mann's Chinese Theatre in Hollywood to Yamashiro restaurant for mounds of expensive sushi.

The Disney premieres are all-day affairs. They are big, expensive circuses with tamed exotic animals roaming Hollywood Boulevard. Children mingle with huge cartoon characters who move among them like vast, careening Technicolor cruise ships. It's a spectacle for the whole family to enjoy, which separates these events from the usual. For the *Tarzan* premiere, the studio built a replica of Tarzan's jungle inside a Hollywood nightclub. There were exotic birds on the shoulders of cheesy models dressed in loincloths. It was a politically incorrect nightmare of chained animals and children tossing brownies to iguanas. But kids got their faces painted by one of the many "Janes" in attendance and a good time was had by all.

Mostly though, the parties are at night and they are usually a pain in the ass for everyone involved. If you are lucky enough to attend as a guest, this is what you can expect: You are herded, like cattle, into a big party space somewhere near the movie theater. During this time most people are thinking about what nice lies they can tell about the movie—which was probably another big-money Hollywood atrocity. Then you have to wait in line for food with all the other hungry industry schmoozers. You'll notice eyes scanning the room, like little darting flashlights shining across a sea of faces, each beady orb looking for an ass to kiss. Then you battle your way across the room, squeezing between young talent agents posing for cameras, hoping they'll make it into George Christie's *Hollywood Reporter* column The Great Life.

There is scant chance that you will find a table because the tables are always reserved for the "talent" and their guests. Of course the talent are still outside making red carpet round number two. Or they are trying to make their way through the blockade of D-girls, agents, and managers who reach out, air kiss, and lie about the movie. So the tables are empty and yet you are crammed up against some flower arrangement in the corner of the room, wondering when the waiter with the chardonnay is going to swing back around. Since you are an assistant, you won't know many of the industry folks by face, only by name and phone number, so it will be nearly impossible to effectively schmooze.

The good news: You'll get some free Wolfgang Puck duck canapés or Mr. Chow's dumplings, you'll get to see a free movie, and have some bragging material for your friends back home.

> *And the Oscar goes to . . .*
> *40 pounds of caviar*
> *25 pounds of black truffles (at $1,000 a pound)*
> *5,400 plates, 6,000 wineglasses*
> *960 bottles of wine*
> *100 pounds of coffee*
> *3,500 yards of gray fleece for the chair covers*
> *About 7,000 orange-red Mercedes roses*
> *225 anthuriums*
> *120 gallons of custom-dyed petroleum oil and 56 pounds of safety glass*
> *used in creating tabletop flower arrangements*
>
> —excerpt from the list of ingredients for the post-Oscars Governors Ball (*Los Angeles Times*, March 24, 2000)

If producing a premiere is like making a movie, producing the Oscars is like making *Titanic*. Chances are, if you are an assistant you will not be attending this glamorous affair. However, if you are an assistant to someone who is nominated, your life will be turned upside down until the last balloon at the last Oscar party pops. As soon as a nomination is announced the flowers pour in, the phone doesn't stop ringing, and the studio starts pressuring your boss to get out there and campaign to win. Reps from all the big designers call and send over catalogues, sketches, and written proposals describing the perfect Oscar gown. As an assistant, you will have to keep track of all of this. Your average workload will double, you'll be scheduling talk show appearances, magazine cover photo approvals, interviews with journalists, not to mention the stacks of scripts that will start pouring in with enthusiastic job offers.

If you are lucky enough to go to the Oscars with your nominated boss, you have to leave your house midafternoon. It takes hours to travel the last few blocks leading to the Shrine auditorium, a hideous structure in the worst part of town. You'll be overdressed for the weather and the entire day and night will be spent holding your bladder like a dog. At the entrance to the Shrine, there are masses of waiting fans mixed with protesters screaming "Hollywood is Babylon!" and that everyone will "burn in hell." Once you get out of the limo you face the longest red carpet of them all, the mother of all red carpets, about fifty yards long and fifty feet wide. Bleachers are set up on both sides, the paparazzi line goes on forever. Joan Rivers is everyone's biggest nightmare. Inevitably, stars must wait their turn to be asked stupifyingly predictable questions by people like Army Archerd, Steve Kmetko, and Roger Ebert and his many chins. Be careful not to get disoriented here, as the flashbulbs and roar of the fans becomes deafening. One star likened the feeling to being on the fifty-yard line at the Astrodome.

An assistant's job on the red carpet is to liaise with your boss's publicist to get the good interviews and help avoid the ones that your boss can afford to snub. The foreign press, for example, might have to take a backseat and so will Fox because, let's face it, chances are Meryl Streep's core audience does not watch *When Good Pets Go Bad.*

The whole event is superlative. It's surreal to be amongst the stars, everywhere you look you see some legend or another, even if it's only Charlton Heston. People dress well, for the most part, and everyone is upbeat and excited. But once the show starts it's long and frequently boring. Everyone is running in and out during the commercial breaks. Seat fillers are dashing in to fill Lara Flynn Boyle's place when she goes to the bathroom every two minutes. You will most likely be sitting way up in the fourth-tier balcony, stiff in your black tie duds, and wishing you were at home eating pizza and making fun of the awful dance numbers with friends.

As you've no doubt noticed, the Academy Awards show takes itself very seriously. Those who have attended often wonder what all the attitude is based upon, since it is one of the worst organized events in Los Angeles. To find your limo after the show is considered an act of divine intervention. Ending the show on time would be enough of a miracle, but how about just managing not to get the ballots and actual statuettes stolen before the show? And expecting the audience to endure Billy Crystal's smug, semiracist humor year after year is more than anyone, even a lowly assistant, should have to bear. One of the more accurate summations of the 2000 show, from Sam Lipsyte in *Feed* magazine:

> They say that Hollywood is high school with money, but last night's Oscars seemed, at times, more like a theater banquet for a small, pricey college. There was Professor Beatty, getting his retirement plaque and rambling on—and on—about responsibility. (They say he used to be quite something with the ladies.) And there were the *American Beauty* folks leaking humanist lubricants all over the podium. And there was Hilary Swank from *Boys Don't Cry* calling for diversity and acceptance in her very own unique, glittery designer dress. Class clown emeritus Billy Crystal kept everything rolling with a few pre-filmed male rape and drag gags and some gentle racial heckling of Best Supporting Physical Anomaly Michael Clarke Duncan. (Funny how the self-serving LAPD joke ended with a cut to the cheerful Duncan, and not to the dignified, soon-to-be-shunned Denzel.) Well, what are you

going to do when the best actor of the lot (Sean Penn) is a no-show and the actor with the best performance of the year (Russell Crowe) looks like a nervous wreck in an aisle seat it's slowly dawning on him he won't need? . . . Maybe the only way to truly understand the Oscars, and the industry they celebrate, is to watch it with your friends and lay some cold hard cash down on the results. With real money riding on the outcome of something you know nothing about—Best Sound Effects Editing, for example—it's possible to appreciate the courage a movie executive must possess to make the kinds of calls that so deeply affect our cultural life. Should you greenlight *The Green Mile*? Should you fast-track *Stuart Little,* pay Spacey what he's asking so he'll do that weird thing with his eyes for you? You must look into your heart and ask, "Who Would Harvey Call"? But the real trick to comprehending how Hollywood works is not just to bet your paycheck on the Oscars, but to lose it. Then you might finally appreciate all the secret sacrifices that have been made to bring you quality distortion and amnesia. Otherwise, to endure the spectacle without taking a quantifiable hit from the contents of the envelope is, to paraphrase the late novelist Stanley Elkin, to be a man in Nebraska told it's raining in France.

Of course people do not really know what it is to put on an awards show, or to endure the hell of making a movie, for that matter. But what they do know is that something smells bad when an overprivileged group of people get together to congratulate themselves while simultaneously trying to upstage one another. In that sense, it can be a momentary relief to be an assistant at one of these award show fiascos, sitting quietly invisible, while the big shots do the sweating for a while.

Then there are the parties afterward, which are nearly impossible to get into. One Academy Award–nominated actress had to fight to get her own mother into the exclusive *Vanity Fair* party at Morton's restaurant. The bouncer actually suggested that the star's mother wait in the parking lot, while the actress attended

the party. Another story comes from the assistant to an actor/
director who received an Oscar nomination. Her boss did not
take her to the Oscar ceremony but did give her a ticket to the
"fabulous" Miramax party. She bought a new dress, got her hair
done at great expense, and spent the whole day getting ready. She
drove to the party but had to park miles away and walk, in heels,
up a steep hill to the Sky Bar on Sunset Boulevard. Finally, she
strutted the red carpet to the velvet rope. She handed over her
ticket only to be turned away by an unforgiving bouncer. It turned
out she had to actually be with her star boss to get in. So the poor
girl had to walk back to her car and sit in traffic forever on
Hollywood's limo-clogged streets. So, if you have any big ideas
about going to the Oscars, make sure you are literally riding in on
someone's coattail.

NYC vs. L.A.:
Central Park vs. Valet Park

Hollywood is a place where people from Iowa mistake each other for a star.

—Fred Allen

The difference between Los Angeles and New York has been talked to death. Without getting into the tired "desert, mountains, beaches" versus "Chinese food at 4 A.M." debate, there are some important distinctions to be made in terms of the entertainment business.

By and large, a Hollywood education can be best obtained in Hollywood, but the right New York job can give you the exposure and the contacts you need to move up. There are fewer jobs in New York and it's much more difficult to live there on an assistant salary. In Hollywood, you will most likely experience full movie business saturation, whereas in New York your friends will have jobs in different fields. This may keep you sane and "in touch" (important in a business catering to the youth market) but it will take you longer to make as many contacts as your West Coast counterparts.

It also depends on what you want to do. If you want to be the next Michael Bay or Joel Silver, you should move to Los Angeles.

If you want to produce the next Ally Sheedy lesbian vehicle, go to New York. New York certainly promotes itself as indie-friendly. To a certain extent this is true, but with costs rising as they are, we can expect the avant-garde to start emerging from such exciting places as Maryland *(Blair Witch Project)*. There are "hip and edgy" production companies, actors, and directors in Los Angeles, too. They usually don't pay as much, but the point is, you don't have to go to New York for the indie experience.

New York is changing so much now that the majority of budding visionaries can't afford island living, and are packing it up for Queens. The whole "street" schtick in New York has gone from break dancing and graffiti to such homogenized franchises as Banana Republic and Disney's Broadway. The cost of living is outrageous and your money flies around without ever seeming to accumulate any material possessions. But that's your money, not the money in the New York movie business. New York movie money is not spent as freely as it is in L.A. The companies are undercapitalized. Or they are smaller operations or simply branch offices who hire only a few employees. It's like this for a reason: there is less money to be made in New York. The great physical production profit margin is in L.A., the land of the soft dollar.

The concept of the industry assistant, as we've described it in this book, doesn't exist as much in New York. Sure, there are the major agency assistants who roll calls and the assistants to bicoastal megalomaniacal producers who shack up in hotels for months at a time. Or assistants to directors, who are usually making a low-budget film that requires your every waking hour. And there are a few studios (mostly satellite offices to cover plays and publishing houses), for which assistants perform the whole L.A. routine, if only for the benefit of their West Coast "people."

For these assistants, there tends to be a much more civilized working environment for the simple reason that in New York folks want to be casual, black-turtleneck-wearing, artistically-inclined-to-sleep-in downtown types. They will wear their bed head with pride. Assistants will work just as hard, it's just that the atmosphere differs from the Hollywood system that encourages a kind of fraternitylike initiation. One that is, as this book has attempted to prove, as much about mental and emotional torture as it is about hard work and long hours.

Authentic New Yorkers would never have their assistant "place a call" and, God forbid, listen in. It's so vulgar and nouveau riche. Like vanity license plates. It's a gross generalization, but it's true that the New Yorker's love of antistatus can make life easier on the underlings.

www.assistant.calm:
The Hollywood Wide Web

Novelty is always welcome but talking pictures are just a fad.
   —Irving Thalberg

Although Hollywood stands to gain billions as film, TV, and Internet technologies advance, most individuals gainfully employed in Tinsel Town have no idea what any of it means or how it really works. It is already a well-established fact that no one in Hollywood reads books, but it is becoming increasingly obvious that even fewer navigate the World Wide Web. Have you seen anything more pathetic than websites for studio movies? They're embarrassing. Many bosses even have their assistants retrieving their e-mail for them. Why is this? Probably because the Web requires patience, the learning of new methodologies, and a willingness to both read and type. These are not aspirations shared by many BMW-driving, Chinese chicken salad eaters.

In fact, it seems the only reason Hollywood has reluctantly faced the challenges presented by the Internet has to do with gossip. Not just the usual Hollywood gossip you can find on sites like E! Online and basically all TV-affiliated dot-coms, but specifically, gossip about movies. The truth is the Internet only grabbed

Hollywood by the balls when anonymous members of the all-important test audiences started posting their reviews of yet-to-be-released films online. If there's anything that can stop traffic on Wilshire Boulevard, it's "bad buzz." And the Internet suddenly provided a forum for "bad buzz" by average moviegoers who had actually seen the studios' product and then shared their opinions with millions of others. What a PR nightmare for the Hollywood machine.

Of course, studios are quickly turning this to their advantage by creating cutesy websites, advertising movies and TV shows, complete with behind-the-scenes photos, footage, and interviews. Internet sweepstakes and websites featuring showtimes and tickets are what the studios want you to click on. What they don't want is you clicking your way into chat rooms about their movies that actually allow people other than Gene Shalit to offer an opinion. In fact, one test screening of Arnold Schwarzenegger's *End of Days* was canceled at the last minute due to the studio's fear that some of the audience members had been solicited to post their thoughts online right after the screening.

Assistants can use the Internet to major advantage in their daily work life. Besides keeping up on industry gossip, often a valuable tool in and of itself, the Web provides easy access to box office results and credits on any given writer, director, producer, or film project . . . even many that have yet to be produced. Good assistants will also use the Web for research on a variety of subjects, from where to send the boss and his mistress for the weekend, to upcoming books with film rights still available. Many story ideas come from television and periodical articles and most of these can now readily be found online. And it is often the great story idea that helps parlay an assistant job into something more.

But before anyone gets too excited about leaving the trenches just yet, we should note that much of an assistant's time online will be spent in more mundane pursuits: ordering bulk Viagra from shady online pharmacies; finding creative gifts for the CAA agent who has everything and whom everyone hates; printing out maps for that difficult four-block drive to Orso; and making air-line reservations under false names so your boss can be assured of an upgrade at the airport.

While we are loath to name many specific websites, since the Net is changing more rapidly than Courtney Love's face, we will mention only one important address here: eBay.com. This massive auction site can help any assistant in a shopping jam. It is also a key place to locate celebrity paraphernalia and to make a tidy profit on those hand-me-downs celebrities inevitably give their assistants.

For the more entrepreneurial, eBay offers a method for a quick turnover for smaller items, like autographed headshots. Rumor has it that Ben Affleck's assistant was auctioning photos to teeny-boppers as fast as the Matt Damon sidekick could sign them.

But why hasn't Hollywood harnessed the Internet boom in a more serious way? There have been a few attempts to put the Web to a more practical Hollywood use. In fact, several people, most notably mogul Steve Tisch, had an idea for a website that would make executives' and producers' lives easier: a site with script coverage. It sounded reasonable to many, the idea of a computer data bank of story synopses and comments by professional script readers. In fact, any writer who received "good coverage" would presumably be thrilled to have the free advertising, right? Well, the literary agents who control the material didn't quite see it that way. In fact, when Tisch and his partners unveiled this idea on the front page of *Variety,* the agents picked up their headsets and called their lawyers and threatened lawsuits. Their argument was that they would be undermined in their effort to sell scripts to studios if negative commentary—or buzz—was already "out there" in the world. They were worried, in effect, that a script could be libeled or slandered. Whether they admitted it or not, the studios could understand the agents' arguments because they were facing the same concerns about their test screenings of bad Schwarzenegger movies.

So the agents prevailed, the coverage website plan was scrapped, and screenplays continue to be sold based on unsubstantiated hype and bidding wars against imaginary "interested parties who've read the great coverage."

On a final note about the Internet, we should answer the most frequently asked question about this topic: Do stars go online? Yes. Most definitely. Stars are online anonymously quite often. In fact the Internet turns out to be the perfect form of communication for these confrontation-shy people who don't really know how to use a phone or have spontaneous contact with other humans. They can e-mail friends, family, and agents instead of returning calls; they can cruise around chat rooms, finally free of the burden of their fame. They chat to others about themselves in the third person, their projects, and people's opinions of them, all protected in a way they never could be out in the world.

Of course, stars have websites, but these are more for their fans. Cyber fans tend to be a specific breed of aggressively stupid teenagers who are obsessed with the cult of personality, but rarely the work of the star. Next time you're online, check out the chat rooms about Jennifer Lopez. We're betting money there's more written about her body and arrest record than her Soderbergh film. Or Leo DiCaprio fans' endless fascination with his sexuality. And you can bet the dumber the fan, the more they write. And the more anger and misdirected rage, the more they write. These people form the core of the Web-user demographics, and it is no surprise that research shows these are the same morons who control Hollywood with their $8.50.

It's Not Just a Job . . . It's an Adventure in Codependency

Yesterday I was a dog. Today I'm a dog. Tomorrow I'll probably still be a dog. Sigh. There's so little hope for advancement.

—Snoopy

As you can see from the stories we've callously delivered unto you, this is a mad, mad, mad, mad world where you are often the conductor of deeply suspect personal and business transactions. It'll make you sick. You'll talk to your friends back home or spend a weekend with nonindustry people, and you'll doubt every decision you've made that brought you to Hollywood. Even if you are a brilliant assistant who comes highly recommended and is ripe for promotion you may, as many have done, pack it up for a more civilized life in another line of work.

Talk to any Hollywood success story and they will have a fully realized fantasy of a simpler life. They dream of being a dog trainer on Nantucket Island, a winemaker in Napa. "Honey, come on, I can't take it, let's start a bed-and-breakfast in Maine. We'll live like normal people, maybe I'll even work for the volunteer fire department and we'll set up a studio so you can get back to your watercolors."

But they rarely do this. And if they do, it's because they've achieved sick amounts of wealth and they can finally live their idyllic country life in style. Consider this while sipping on Francis Ford Coppola's latest vintage.

WHERE'S THE ROMANCE?

So what does it really take to dive into this world, you ask? Well, if you are the child of divorced parents and had to take care of one or both of them, then you are well prepared for this job. If you tend toward abusive relationships, a bonus. You have Daddy-pleasing issues? You're hired. Draw on whatever childhood trauma you've suffered in order to dredge up the emotional juice it takes to handle this job. The relationship between a boss and his assistant is emotionally destructive. You trade in your life for theirs. You live to make their life livable.

The very best assistants are really in love with their bosses. The suppression of this crush can yield wonderful results in the workplace. Think of that psychotic girl in high school English class who had a crush on the teacher. She may have ended up in the psych ward, but chances are she got straight A's. Or better yet, think of the ideal wife of the fifties, propping a pillow behind her husband's head as he reclines with the *Evening Post.* That wife knows more about her husband's needs than he does: "Remember, sweetie, crab cakes give you gas"; "Your wallet is in the pocket of your brown slacks that are draped over the back of the bedroom chair." This is the stuff a dream assistant is made of.

You retain more information when you have a vested interest. You'll be most likely to remember that your boss's girlfriend hates gladiolas because her ex-husband used to buy them for his mistress, that he hates onions unless they're heavily sautéed in butter and not oil, that when people end words with the suffix "-ish" he immediately thinks they're stupid. You'll remember this trivia painlessly if you are secretly in love with him.

The reverse can be true. You can work from a place of pure hatred . . . but it's not as fun. This strategy is one of competition and rebellion, more like that from teenager to strict parents. "I'm going to show them. I'm going to do such a good job, I'm going to know more about their lives than they do, I'm going to make them dependent on me. They will become the prisoner of my scheduling, of my phone sheets; without me, they're nothing." Vindictiveness is a draining lifestyle, but then again, so is a schoolgirl crush.

We're not actually suggesting that you try to achieve this twisted relationship if it's not there. But chances are it will develop, so it's important to maintain a functioning, codependent relationship with your boss.

Another upsetting side effect of the assistant/boss relationship occurs when the boss uses the assistant to fill a vacuum in his or her own life. And Hollywood is destination numero uno for those seeking to fill a vacuum. It's not uncommon for bosses to call their assistants with nothing in particular to say or demand. They are just lonely workaholics who've given up a chance for a real relationship to make it in this highly competitive business, so the minute they are alone without work they are at a complete loss. This is ultimately a very depressing peek into your boss's isolated, alienated psyche and for a moment you might have sympathy, but that will quickly disappear when you show up at work on Monday and that same lonely person has moved back into his more per-manent mode of operation: that of cold, mercurial taskmaster.

Just remember that when an entire film crew witnesses a fully grown, successful producer screaming like a five-year-old at his twenty-two-year-old assistant, they are probably going to identify with the assistant. Who looks stupid when the boss throws the cell phone at the kid, who ducks, and then watches it roll under the wheels of a passing truck? When he starts blaming the assis-tant, you can bet that he's the one who looks like a fool.

So when (not if) you screw up something, even if it's just for-getting to remind the gardener not to sing while he's working because it makes the pool boy "nervous," just remember the many who have gone before you down this long, dark hallway and come out alive.

To this end, one of our favorite stories is that of Karen Fields, who worked as one of five assistants to producer Joel Silver. At some point there was a pot-bellied pig in the office. Karen's job was to walk the pig. To stand around the Warner Bros. lot, waiting for the pig to defecate. She felt humiliated and stupid. As of the writing of this book, she's planning the renovations to their enormous Brentwood estate, as Joel's fiancée.

TRADING UP: WHAT COMES NEXT

The lunatics have taken charge of the asylum.
—United Artists Film Corp., 1920

An assistant job typically lasts a year or two. And that is generally a good amount of time to figure out what you want your next step to be, inside or outside of your current company. In addition, you will have more leverage within the company if you have now made yourself indispensable. You're the only one who knows where the files are, the only one who knows which is the latest draft of a script, and where to find Madonna's private number.

However, if you do not wish to stay at the same place, you should have a definite sense of what it is you want to do by now. Only by making it clear—and easy—for those around you to help you in your move will you be able to garner the support and favors that are a necessary part of career promotion within the industry.

LIFE AFTER DEATH

Just as the way into your first job in Hollywood is paved with time-honored traditions, so is the way up to your next job. There can be

potholes along the road, particularly if you do not leave your current
job on good terms. So remember the golden rule of quitting: Always
find your replacement. This will mean putting the word out among
fellow assistants, placing ads in the trades, listing the job opportunity
on the big corporate e-mail rosters, and spending significant time
fielding calls and screening candidates.

We've spent a lot of time explaining what a Hollywood assistant needs to watch out for. Now it's time to discuss what a
Hollywood assistant has to look forward to. While there are the
occasional rags-to-riches stories of people like Harrison Ford,
who was a carpenter who got discovered remodeling some film-
maker's house, most Hollywood success stories feature hard work
and good timing. It's worth repeating that in Hollywood, luck is
preparation meeting opportunity.

Most assistants move up by jumping ship, not through promotions within companies. And those who find the next, great job
tend to put out feelers early and discreetly. No one wants an
employee who seems desperate and yaks to anyone and everyone
about how anxious they are to "escape" their current situation.
The most effective way to get hired on elsewhere consists of a
time-honored Hollywood tradition: get someone else to put you
up for the job. The attitude should be one of: Hey, I'm not even
looking because I'm such a loyal, hard worker who is greatly
appreciated by all who work with me. Let the potential new boss
think it's his idea, albeit slipped to him by a colleague (the colleague is your advocate in the situation, to whom you've promised
undying gratitude if he'll throw your name in the hat).

And when you do (discreetly) secure the new position, make
sure you don't burn bridges with your psycho boss. His biggest
concern will probably be finding out if you'll blab about his creepy
behavior, so assure him you won't. Maybe even offer to sign a
confidentiality agreement if you haven't already (just be prepared
to stick to it).

If, as you leave the office at 11 P.M. for the fifth night this
week, you start to doubt the possibilities of ever moving up the

food chain, keep in mind the following recent examples of people who worked hard and did well:

Amy Pascal started as an assistant to a producer, worked as a development executive, and now she's the chairman of Columbia Pictures. She has mentored others, like:

. . . Michael Costigan, who wisely started as an assistant to a producer at Witt-Thomas Films during his college summer breaks (Hollywood likes 'em young). When he applied for a creative executive job at Columbia, having carefully memorized a list of recent Columbia hit movies, he accidentally blurted out how much he loved *My Own Private Idaho*, which he had seen the previous night. The accidental honesty landed him the job, and he "was encouraged by Amy, who taught me to fight for ideas I really loved." This led Michael to champion the oddball pitch by two relatively unknown writers, which later became *The People vs. Larry Flynt.* Just a few years after leaving his assistant job, Michael was promoted to the level of vice president at Columbia. A story similar to that of his fellow Brown alum:

. . . Elysa Koplovitz, a young woman who served as assistant to former top Warner Bros. exec Mark Canton. She stayed loyal to her boss as he moved from Warners to Columbia and now she's risen to the level of VP at MTV Films, where she works on projects at Paramount with:

. . . Dee Dee Gardner, who began her life in the biz as an assistant to Joanie Evans, a major New York book agent. Within a few short years, she landed a job at Paramount as VP of production, where she does business with agents like:

. . . Richard Lovett, who worked as an assistant to CAA's Fred Spector. Lovett is now among the top brass at CAA, which sells product to:

. . . Kevin Misher, current president of Universal. He cut his teeth as studio chief Mike Medavoy's assistant. Now he buys scripts from writers like:

. . . Callie Khouri, who, while assisting an agent, wrote and sold *Thelma and Louise* for six figures. She's now one of the most sought-after writers in town, pursued by executives like:

. . . USA Films' Kerry Foster, who went from assisting a literary agent at CAA, to a vice presidency at Barry Diller's newly formed film studio, practically overnight. She's twenty-seven, just a few years younger than:

. . . Adam Chase, who started in Hollywood fresh out of college as an assistant to agent Susan Smith. While there, working for $350 per week, he wrote some sample TV episodes of *The Simpsons* and got noticed by Jim Brooks. Jim hired him as a PA at his Gracie Films and he had the distinct honor of driving Mr. Brooks around in a golf cart on the Columbia/Tri-Star lot. Adam managed to get his scripts read and was put on staff for a failed show about a child tennis prodigy. But it wasn't long before he started writing a new little show called *Friends* for NBC. Six years later, he's on the front page of the trade papers, announcing his new $14 million development deal. He's come a long way from the days he shared a cramped office with:

. . . Rick Yorn, who had just arrived in L.A. from New Jersey. After a few months of working for a lit agent at Susan Smith, he began to assist Susan herself, working with actors. He then went to work for a talent manager, Phyllis Carlyle, and quickly parlayed his relationships with young actors, like one young kid on *Growing Pains* (Leonardo DiCaprio) into a partnership with Michael Ovitz, founding a new management company: AMG.

So, as you can see, there is a bright side. And while the world will continue to be full of demanding employers and unfair hierarchies, the Hollywood assistant can exit boot camp secure in the knowledge that he or she can weather any storm. And just to make sure you understand why no assistant ever looks back nostalgically, we'll leave this chapter with a fitting anecdote from the assistant to a powerful studio executive:

When his doctor requested that he come in to give a stool sample, he wanted to save time, so he gave me a Tupperware container with the, uh, sample inside it. I was supposed to hand deliver this thing to the doctor's office. I couldn't believe it. And he could tell I was shocked, even though I was trying to play it cool. Then he looked me in the eye and said, "This is the most important thing you'll ever do."

Frequently Annoying Questions

Q: How come everyone in Hollywood has so much money, except me?

A: First of all, don't let appearances deceive you. Often, it seems as though everyone you work for, and the people they deal with, and all of the players you read about in the trades, and all of the slick assholes you see valet parking their cars in front of you at Lucques, have unlimited financial resources. But in Hollywood, chances are the car is leased, as is the gaudy house in the hills, and the lavish lifestyle is underwritten by expense accounts and credit cards rising dangerously close to their high limits. Sure, there is a lot of money to be made in the industry and there are plenty of twenty-something millionaires to prove it. But these screenwriters, actors, directors, and producers are a lot like Lotto winners—they squander their once-in-a-lifetime payday on ostentatious purchases and loser relatives and soon find themselves borrowing heavily to keep up the expected lifestyle in between big hits.

A perfect example would be a certain young screenwriter we know, who, after years of living hand-to-mouth on money borrowed from his parents, sold a spec script to a major studio for a cool $1.2 million. Amazing, right? This guy must be set for life, you're thinking. All his friends celebrated his long-awaited triumph. We went to lavish parties thrown at the trendiest Beverly Hills restaurants, he acquired a $75,000 car, rented a million-dollar house in the hills from an A-list director, took major vacations, spent another thirty grand on furniture and electronics, filled his closet with black-label Armani, hired a business manager who charged him 5 percent of his annual income (on top of the 5 percent going to his lawyer), gave generous gifts to friends and family (including the world's most expensive set of golf clubs to Dad), hired a health food delivery service to deliver all his meals daily, hired a dog walker and a masseuse, and got engaged.

Now keep in mind that 10 percent of his "winnings" already went to his agents, and another 15 percent to his manager. Did we mention the Writers Guild? Legally, he had to join, since the studio is a signatory to the Guild. That's a few thousand right there. Then our screenwriter friend had to pay at least $12,000 more in Guild dues. All this before being hit with his tax bill, now showing him suddenly among the wealthiest Americans, and therefore now in the 40 percent tax bracket, not including state taxes. And, his well-paid attorney informed him, he needed to spend thousands more to incorporate himself. The net result? Let's just say, within a year he was scrambling to sell another script.

But back to you. The reason why you, as the assistant, may still be making only relative pennies even after a few years toiling for others has to do with psychological warfare as well as capitalist market economics. You see, if the powers that be can keep you hungry, starving just outside the gates of their Santa Monica faux–Mediterranean villas, watching them feast on sashimi-grade ahi tuna seared and served over a bed of white truffle–infused seasonal field greens, they've got you right where they want you. You're hooked. Working ninety-hour weeks and suffering at the injustice of it all, but nonetheless determined to work even harder to achieve your own personal fantasy of the good life.

At the same time, you must realize that the law of supply and demand is at work here like nowhere else. You, the assistants of the world, are in copious supply and demand is limited. And the money is really used to entice the big fish, the sure moneymakers, into the fold and to keep them there. And not just movie stars. TV writer/producers are now being lured into obscenely rich studio pacts in what is a testament to the limitless slot machine of series television. Recently, David E. Kelley *(The Practice, Ally McBeal)* signed a contract north of $100 million, which does not even include the rights to his priceless feature projects, such as *Lake Placid*. We doubt his assistant earns even the equivalent of his Writers Guild dues (1 percent).

Q: **Will I be expected to run lots of personal errands for my boss?**

A: It depends. More than in most industries, Hollywood assistants are generally asked to do a considerable amount of personal stuff for employers. This tends to be even more true if you're working for a noncorporate type, like an actor, writer, independent producer, etc. Studio and network executives, as well as lawyers and other button-down types, seem to respect work boundaries and personal boundaries in a slightly more traditional fashion. Often, this is mandated by corporate policy to avoid liability. For instance, Sony doesn't really want to pay the whiplash bill if you're rear-ended en route to the pharmacy for your VP's monoxydil.

The extent to which you're a personal slave can also be mitigated by dealing with the issue up front, during job negotiations. If you really think you'll break out in hives if asked to go to the dry cleaners, then say so. Sometimes, this will be a less important aspect of an employer's requirements. But frequently, you'll find that an assistant's ability to take care of personal business with competence and grace may be the top priority for the boss. "Anyone can answer the phone," is the attitude of many a mogul too busy to meet the contractor at the Malibu horse ranch.

And time is what it really boils down to. After all, it's not that these control freaks really want you to know about their personal foibles and necessities; or that they actually trust you to get the right rawhide chew toys for their yellow Labradors, it's that they don't have the time to do it themselves. Chances are, if you don't see the personal stuff as a demeaning nightmare, they won't either, and their respect and appreciation for you might actually blossom with each flu-buster smoothie you land on their desks.

Q: **What's the deal with publicists?**

A: Once associated solely with stars, publicists now cater to directors, writers, even producers. As an assistant, you will most likely have to deal with publicists in both positive and negative situations. Even if your immediate boss does not employ a publicist (they generally cost clients at least $2,000 to $3,000 per month), they will probably represent talent or even a film with which your boss is involved. Hence, you will be on the phone with the office of the publicist invariably begging for premiere tickets, party invitations, or invites to any other events they arrange.

On the other hand, publicists also exist to hassle your boss to do press interviews on behalf of their clients. And if you work for one of the publicists' actual clients, you may find yourself saying "no" to the infinite publicity requests, putting yourself at odds with these often rabidly aggressive promoters. But there are also a fair number of classy publicity types who know how to throw great events, protect their clients' privacy, and simultaneously achieve the desired public perception for the client. These are the ones who really earn their salaries. It will behoove you to learn who they are early on.

Q: How is religion viewed in Hollywood?

A: As you well know, money, power, and fame are the gods of show business. Aside from that, your pagan beliefs are not of much importance to others, or to your career. There do not seem to be many devout anythings in Hollywood, and frankly, it is hard to imagine people who don't honor their own deal memos keeping their pacts with God.

If you are a practicing Jew, you should feel comfortable in a business that boasts a relatively large percentage of Jewish executives and practically no anti-Semitic sentiment within the industry (except for casting directors fond of the phrase "too Jewish"). There are a few Catholics running around, too, but they seem to get invited to many more seders than Easter dinners.

The hot topic in religion, of course, is Scientology. Now we're sure you've heard and read plenty about this controversial religion started by sci-fi author L. Ron Hubbard. Like everything else in Hollywood, it's probably half rumor and lies, and the other half gossip. Critics of Scientology claim it's a brainwashing, materialistic, self-centered cult that preys upon the weakest in Hollywood, like insecure and/or chemically dependent, self-hating, homosexual actors. Supporters portray it as a legitimate, evolved, spiritual path to self-realization and self-activation, unfettered by the hypocritical and outdated trappings of traditional organized religion. Whatever you may feel about this Hollywood-based organization, just know that they've got a ton of money and perceived power, with members like Tom Cruise, John Travolta, Kirstie Alley, and at least one studio owner, ready to go to bat against any detractors. And the Church of Scientology (located just down the street from Ripley's "Believe It or Not" Museum in Hollywood) is notoriously litigious. So as an assistant, think carefully before you offer up your personal opinions on this one.

Q: What about all of my graduate degrees? Don't they count for anything?

A: No. Not at first, anyway. In fact, there are many lawyers and MBAs who start as assistants to agents or producers as a matter of course. The entertainment industry is its own unique little training ground, and even Harvard law graduates know they need to go to boot camp Hollywood.

That is not to say, however, that advanced degrees won't come in handy later on, as you ascend the ranks. Particularly in corporations like studios and agencies, these degrees can be valued by the "elders" as they decide whom to promote and how far you can go. To this end, many agents have benefited from having MBA and/or law degrees. And these really are the two most valued degrees in Hollywood, no matter what you've heard about film schools, MFAs, and producing programs. Naturally, these qualifications are job-specific. Want to run TV operations in Peru? Then maybe your Latin American studies will pay off. Otherwise, don't count on it.

Keep in mind that in this industry, where dreams really do come true, education can play almost no role whatsoever in terms of your success. One respected producer who has a swank deal with a major studio was a high school dropout. And when he tells you this, while flitting between meetings and lunches with the biggest Hollywood talent, he does so with a hint of self-congratulation.

Q: My best friend is a struggling actor/writer/director who wants me to help him/her. What do I do?

A: Okay, this can be the biggest nightmare of all. If you've been drawn to this "creative" business, chances are you have close friends who are "creative" types as well. We feel your pain. Inevitably, they are needy and desperate, somewhat talented but not really star material, and they just need you to do them this one favor or make this one phone call and it's definitely the last time they'll ask you but, hey, you know people and they don't know anyone and they're going to die unknown due to your unbelievably selfish behavior if you don't exploit what few connections you have to help them immediately.

This is generally what we call a no-win situation for the put-upon assistant and here's why. First, no one wants an assistant who puts his boss on the spot to do school chums a favor, no matter how good they were in *Ah, Wilderness!* senior year. You've got Cuba Gooding Jr. dying to come in and meet? Great, send him in. Otherwise, leave me alone and leave the talent scouting to the casting directors.

"So should I use my boss's name and call a casting director?" No, you imbecile! Have you learned nothing here? Most casting directors will be smart enough to figure out that if your boss really wanted them to pay attention to the *Ah, Wilderness!* star, he would have called himself.

Second, even if you do have some substantial clout with your boss or others who might be in a position to help your friend, do you really want to squander it by making a request that won't really amount to anything? Sure, you can ask to get your actor/writer/director friend an audition/interview/meeting, but no one's going to actually hire him or her based on your recommendation alone. Somewhere along the line, Ah, Wilderness! has to deliver the goods himself and why should you take the fall along with him when he chokes?

"But what if he turns out to be the next Jason Priestley?" you naively ask, already planning your summers at his Malibu Colony beach house, just a stone's throw from whatever neighbor's bed Robert Downey Jr. is currently facedown in. Well, smarty-pants, if Ah, Wilderness! turns out indeed to be a legend of both stage and screen, rest assured no one's going to credit an unknown assistant with the discovery.

Third, you are not really doing Ah, Wilderness! a favor when you beg others to take an interest in him. After all, actors and directors usually have a "reel" (their badly duped VHS tape showing their wares) so their work can be judged on its own merits, at least to a certain degree. And writers have scripts to be read. The executive, agent, manager, casting director, or whomever else you'd like to impress will probably end up annoyed by the extra lobbying efforts, and a little red flag will go up saying, in effect, "If Ah, Wilderness! is so gifted, why does he need people trying to get him in the back door?" Good question.

Fourth, in the long run you are only starting a cycle of codependence, into which you will be dragged deeper and deeper, until serious, friendship-threatening fights can erupt. This happens more often than you'd think. And even when friendships aren't damaged, careers can be. One assistant tried to help an old college friend by coercing the agent he worked for to sign the actor against her will. Years later, as nothing was happening in the actor's career and the assistant now worked for a manager, the assistant was asked to intervene again. So the assistant got the manager to represent the actor as well. Naturally, nothing happened, despite the notable representation, and the actor may have wasted valuable time that could have been better spent with a smaller agency that believed in him.

Finally, in the long run, it is to the advantage of all artists in the Hollywood system to be able to administrate their own careers and learn to rely on their own talent, rather than feeling beholden to connections and nepotism. Most Hollywood "insiders" would probably tell you that, with a few notable exceptions, "connections" at the assistant/junior level don't mean much in the reality of the marketplace.

Q: Do writers hire assistants?

A: There are hotshot writers, like Ron Bass, who not only have personal assistants but also sometimes even a whole team of writing assistants (Bass's are known as the "Ronettes") who help him with his daily dozens of polishes, rewrites, and adaptations of such pieces as *Stepmom*. However, generally speaking, only A-list writers have assistants. For one thing, they can afford to. The younger writers, who are trying to build a career in the risky and competitive world of selling scripts, would be foolish to dole out money for someone to run all the errands, errands that are usually welcome excuses for a frustrated writer to get out of the house and away from the computer screen, which is most likely covered with files titled "movie ideas," "ideas," "character ideas," "pilot ideas."

There are some writers who realize that they simply cannot function without an assistant. They are creative, after all. They must get so deeply immersed in the world of their movie that they don't have the time to be in their "own shoes." They are too "involved" to pay bills, or to stock up on ink cartridges, or to put the lid back on the peanut butter. These mad artists will acquire an assistant, but usually only on a casual or part-time basis. One Hollywood writer was in such a deep fit of anxiety over an extremely overdue script for a major diva to star in, he hired an assistant to bring him a bowl of Jerry's famous matzoh-ball soup, from all the way across town, each day at noon.

If you want to be a writer and you have a fantasy of working for the latest screenwriting sensation, helping them with ideas and plot points and spelling, as they mentor you through your first years in "final draft," forget it. You won't be sitting in the sparsely decorated glass house, on the top of some Hollywood hill, smoking pot with the next William Goldman as he listens intently to your take on the ending of his latest draft.

There is one writer, however, who got an introduction to Hollywood like no other. How this polite, cable-knit-vested, WASP, twenty-two-year-old from Bethesda, Maryland, ended up visiting Robert Downey Jr. in jail to do "script notes" only a year after moving to L.A. is a script idea in itself.

Peter grew up spending weekends at "the club" where he and his father would golf and then share polite conversation over shrimp cocktails and ham sandwiches. He slept his way through an Ivy League education, watched a lot of TV, barely graduated and then wrote what he describes as his "modern-day *Chinatown*." He moved to Los Angeles to become the next Robert Towne. He drove all the way across country to a place where he knew only one person, an ex-girlfriend of his older brother's. She had a career as a writer so he called her for advice. She read his script and believed it to be promising, gave him notes, and her agent's phone number. But most important, she turned him on to another writer who was falling apart under a deadline and needed help for a few hours each day. Peter was hired.

He made a terrible assistant. One afternoon, his boss called in desperation, "Do you remember the files of all my business expenses for 1997? I've been looking for them for weeks, I've turned the house upside down, do you have any recollection as to where they might be?" Peter responded casually, "Oh yeah, they're in the back of my car."

He would go all the way to Kinko's to xerox something and then realize he'd forgotten it and have to drive back. One thing Peter could do was cook. So the writer ended up simply doing his errands himself while his assistant stayed home and prepared rack of lamb with baby potatoes or grilled swordfish. The two of them ended up having long, wonderful lunches, but after a while the writer realized he was getting less work done than before.

One day the writer gets a call from an old friend, an eccentric, hippy geezer living in Topanga Canyon where he practices naked yoga and meditation in between gigs as a character actor in small movies and commercials. He calls because he and Robert Downey Jr., who became friends on the set of *Less Than Zero,* have decided to write a script together about Robert's life and they need an assistant to "help with the typing." So the writer recommends Peter and trades in the pleasure of poached salmon with dill for his former, more productive, lifestyle.

So our young hero meets the hippy geezer actor and Robert Downey Jr. They agree on an hourly wage and meet each day between eleven and three. At first the "typist" did just what he was told. He kept quiet, in part because he was just the secretary, but also because he knew nothing of the world these two actors were describing. You see, Peter had never even taken a puff of pot, much less anything close to the kind of experiences Robert was recounting. He would sit there studiously noting anecdotes and every now and then asking something like, "So, dope is heroin, right? Not coke?"

But soon Peter began suggesting things and Robert and the geezer liked them. Then he was taking the day's conversations and recycling them, from the minitape-recorded sessions, into pages. He became the conductor of the chaos and the two official writers began to defer to Peter; "Let's ask what Pete thinks," they would say when there was a disagreement. At one point Robert said, "Well, let's ask Peter, he's writing the goddamned thing." By the time they finished the script, Peter was officially credited as the third writer and the three had become a wonderfully odd group of friends.

They were three very different people, yet they worked together brilliantly, playing off one another, exploiting the range of experience they collectively brought to the room, and working the tension among the three generations. A kid, a dad, and a geezer. And they wrote a wonderful script. Now Peter is working on a variety of projects based on this initial, successful collaboration. He got an agent out of the deal, lots of advice, a heap of working experience, and a little bit more than just an hourly wage.

Q: **I'm also a writer. How do I get my script read?**
A: Of course you're also a writer. Who isn't? In Hollywood, where assistants read and witness horrible scripts selling for big bucks every day, everyone with a word processor is screenwriting. To not do so would be tantamount to living in a trailer park and not playing the lottery.

The hard part is getting your script read and considered in a serious fashion, given that you are, in fact, one of the thousands of assistants trying to trade up. With that in mind, here are a few tips that might help.

Your illustrious authors, Ceridwen and Bill, both sold screenplays while serving as assistants. Ceridwen cleverly used a pseudonym for her sale to Miramax, thereby eliminating any of the "oh, it's a script written by an assistant" prejudice that often exists within production companies and studios. True, her nom de plume was "Carey Rockefeller," but at least no one associated her script with "that idiotic girl who always disconnects me when she tries to put me on hold."

The first step in submitting your 120-page masterpiece is getting an agent. Most companies will not read "unsolicited material" (scripts that don't come from an agent/manager/lawyer) for legal reasons. So how do you get an agent to represent your opus? Usually through friendly allies who agree to pass it on. For example, Bill, the producer of Ceridwen's script, had submitted it to some agent friends at William Morris. Thanks to her inspired pseudonym, Ceridwen didn't need to worry that competitive fellow assistants would "accidentally" lose pages in the copier or spill coffee on the last act. And the agents were all the more intrigued by the thought of a "new writer" they might be able to sign. They said "yes" to Ms. Rockefeller.

Of course, the script was good, too. That always helps. And it fetched a large sum on the open market, weeks later. Ceridwen was also wise to have a writing partner who could carry the ball when Ceridwen was too busy or exhausted from her more than full-time job. Writing partners can be an assistant's best friend, if chosen carefully. When Bill sold his script to Disney, he had a partner who was a more experienced screenwriter and who had the added advantage of already being represented by two of the top literary agents in the business. On the other hand, Bill chose to discontinue writing with a fellow slave when they were starting out at an agency, just before the guy got the job running *Friends*—so why listen to him?

In addition to writing partners, aspiring screenwriters should cultivate any and all connections to agents and literary managers. These can be more important than studio contacts, because most studio executives don't feel comfortable buying material, even that they like, if it wasn't submitted by an agent. And remember, even friends can be given your work "anonymously." Tear off the title page and you'll be surprised what honest feedback you can get.

Q: **What's the attitude toward homosexuality? What if my . . . uh . . . uh . . . friend is gay?**

A: In a radical departure from the usual tone of this book, for once we will not insult your intelligence by explaining that many artistic types are gay and hence, Hollywood itself is just one big rainbow-colored quilt, filled with politically correct Saab convertible drivers, currently in training for the next AIDS Ride. Besides, it's not really true.

Like everywhere else in America, gays are ghettoized in Hollywood, albeit their segregation takes place in the gilded cages of trendy West

Hollywood clubs, Gold's gym, and parties thrown in the hills by the "velvet mafia."

This is not to say that much discrimination takes place within the business itself. After all, there are openly gay studio owners, heads of production, agency and studio VPs, managers, directors, producers, and "character actors." And the straights, for the most part, are enlightened in their acceptance of gays into the family. At least on the surface. As one of the most successful producers in town said recently, "It's great to have homosexuals working for you. They don't have families, they work long hours, and they're devoted and reliable."

This kind of dubious appreciation has not prevented gays from thriving in the entertainment industry, although many seem to bump their heads on a glass ceiling of sorts. Like straight women, gay men and lesbians can often rise to the titular level of "president of production" but rarely do they ascend beyond, to the CEO and chairman levels. Similarly, with the singular exception of Anne Heche, no leading actors are openly gay and this continues to be the ultimate taboo.

Of course, in the land where people fall over themselves to be "hip and edgy," many Hollywood types pride themselves on their association with those living the "alternative lifestyle." But, to paraphrase John Gregory Dunne, "the Hollywood rule is to act gay and be straight."

Q: How important is it for me to watch movies and TV?

A: Chances are that as an assistant you will not be asked for in-depth analysis of current films and television. Even during the interview process, as we've mentioned, you probably won't be asked to go much deeper than "what's your favorite movie?"

Nonetheless, it's a good idea to have a working knowledge of box office and TV rating hits, as well as some references to "the classics." This is not merely a good idea in the sense that you might actually sound informed about the very career path that you've chosen. But you will most definitely find it helpful to have points of comparison from which to draw when writing coverage of new material or when asked to summarize a script's or treatment's viability.

It is not necessary to be fluent only in the masters. In fact, there is hardly a duller sight in Hollywood than some kid in the mail room holding forth on Stanley Kubrick's "final, haunting masterpiece." Scorsese's a genius? Gee, hold on while we alert the press. Remember, you're more valuable to prospective employers if you keep your nose to the ground and sniff out the new breed, the up-and-comers, the faces that are sure to grace the cover of *Film Threat* tomorrow.

Q: I'm paranoid, bipolar, and can't afford therapy. Am I alone?

A: No. Not at all. The only difference between you and your boss in this regard is that your boss can afford the shrink. The ever-expanding waves of depression and anxiety that normally engulf young twenty-somethings are even more pronounced among the alienated, mistreated neophytes of Wilshire Boulevard. Adding to the mental health crisis in Beverly Hills and surrounding areas is the cruel paradox that many assistant jobs don't carry health benefits. And those that do often exclude mental health coverage altogether, or have high deductibles and low maximum benefits. And if you suffer from SAD (seasonal affective disorder) in the winter, well, try and get a corner office (with nonopening windows).

Our helpful hints are pretty basic: invest in a dysfunctional family-size bottle of Saint-John's-wort, get a low-maintenance pet, plenty of sunshine, exercise and meditate a lot, and go to the beach and mountains whenever possible. Other than that, excessive drinking, drugging, eating, mindless sex, and shopping are other popular alternatives.

Q: Where do I go to detox?

A: After about six months on the job, you will undoubtedly feel toxic. Not just from the harsh words, vitriolic atmosphere, and morally bankrupt office setting, but quite literally from the toxins you will consume each weekend, if not nightly. Most assistants drink, many heavily, at least half the women smoke, and drug use among assistants is rampant.

So where do you go when it all catches up to you? Since you won't be able to afford Betty Ford on your Newt Gingrich budget, try some local R&R when the going gets tough. For instance, Beverly Hot Springs is an ideal Koreatown day spa for serious soaking, steaming, and shiatsu. In New York, try Bliss.

After your Christmas bonus, think about heading to Two Bunch Palms, outside of Palm Springs. Serious mud baths, desert meditation, and natural hot springs swimming pools. Or the Ritz in Laguna or Palm Springs for a weekend of decadence and breakfast in bed.

Just a few more hours by car is the amazing Big Sur, off the Pacific Coast Highway in Northern California. Breathtaking scenery and good food await the crumbling assistant. Or try the Arizona desert or a weekend trip to Mexico—Baja is especially satisfying for beachgoers. Just be sure to avoid the ever-tempting Las Vegas if you're serious about detoxing.

Of course, the ultimate "free-tox" is a trip home to the parents, or "Chez Nightmare" as we like to call it. This is your best bet for nutritious food, enforced substance abuse codes, and a good night's sleep. If you want to stay in town, try a quick fix at Burke-William's day spa in L.A., or YogaWorks in Santa Monica. Hike the canyons, Rollerblade at the beach. After all, you might as well take advantage of the few good points L.A. has to offer.

As for New Yorkers, leaving early on Fridays is practically in the job description. And, if you can find a friend with a house in the Hamptons, Fire Island, or anywhere outside of Manhattan go, go, go. You need the perspective (even if it comes in the form of falling asleep in front of the Sunday game while reclining on your uncle's La-Z-Boy in his split-level on the outskirts of Bergenfield, New Jersey).

Q: God took the seventh day off, can I?

A: Yes. Unless you're in an agency trainee program and you're delivering scripts and trying to do lots of reading to brownnose your way on to a desk. In that case, probably not. But for the most part, employers encourage their assistants to relax when they have downtime. Not because anyone actually cares about your well-being, but they'd rather have you rested and perky when the espresso hits the fan on Monday. One notable exception is the infamous line attributed to workaholic Jeffrey Katzenberg when he was at Disney: "If you don't come in on Saturday, don't bother showing up on Sunday." According to ancient folklore (a.k.a., *Vanity Fair*), when employees, working overtime, reminded Katzenberg it was Christmas Eve, he responded, "So let's order turkey sandwiches."

For your part, organize your free time well and make sure you get to recharge your batteries. No one wants an assistant who's worked all weekend and rolls in tired and frazzled and cranky. Or an assistant who's partied all weekend and rolls in hungover and useless. And if you can't unwind, try the shooting range in the valley. Joe Mantegna or Charlton Heston's assistant should be able to point you in the right direction.

Q: **Don't you guys have any uplifting stories about assistants?**
A: Okay. Here's a story about Lester, a slightly dysfunctional but brilliant kid who saved an agent from using clichés by being her Cyrano for a day.

Lester has a job as an assistant at a high-profile entertainment law firm in Los Angeles. Lester has an unbelievable well of knowledge, he's an encyclopedia, a poet, and a visionary. But Lester does a lot of acid. He smokes a lot of pot. He doesn't have a car. He doesn't have a watch. He doesn't have an e-mail account. He doesn't have a cell phone. He has a wonderful, lyrical way of speaking. He is the antiassistant.

Lester is operating from a place of trippy, hippy, enlightened, abstracted order. He is a mess. But his boss and everyone at the law firm loves him. They invite him to every party, they stay up all night listening to his ecstatic theories about Thomas Jefferson or the history of the court jester, and let it slide when he botches a simple errand.

One day, the high-powered lit agent wife of one of the law partners calls her husband and says, "One of my clients is premiering her movie in London and I need a good quote for a note I'm sending with flowers. Her movie is a period piece so I need something, like Shakespearean, something classy." So her husband calls Lester into his office and asks him if he can think of anything.

Lester says, "Can I borrow the keys to your car?"

"Sure."

"I'll be right back."

Lester disappears to his apartment for about an hour and returns, a bit frazzled. He calls the agent and reads to her the following poem:

When through the fearsome fray you've come,
And find your work to be well done
The thunderous cry of the crowd pours free,
There is a voice that speaks for me.

She loves it. They hang up and Lester is the hero. But then she calls back and asks her husband, "My assistant just pointed out to me, I have to credit the quote, I have to say who said it." So he calls Lester in, "Who wrote it?"

Lester stands there panicked and then turns red and looks at his feet. "I did. I'm sorry, it's just that I couldn't find anything that was right, so I just wrote it." His boss laughed, amazed at Lester's internal resources, and said, "Don't worry, it's brilliant, we'll just say it's 'Anonymous, seventeenth century' and leave it at that."

Lester just wrote a script and you can bet the lit agent is representing it.

Q: **What if my boss wants to have a heart-to-heart about "us"?**
A: Sitting down with your boss for a cozy tête-à-tête can be a lot like exiting the highway at a rest area: either it provides welcome relief from the monotony and hardship of the journey or you'll end up getting mugged and stabbed.

Some enlightened employers may actually care enough to "check in" and discuss the working relationship you share. If they are sincere, this can be the perfect time to address issues of salary, working conditions, environment, responsibilities, hours, benefits, etc. However, more often than not, these conversations turn out to be more like monologues (we call them "bosso-logues," consisting of whiny executives or stars enumerating their ever-increasing needs and your ever-increasing shortcomings). It is usually just another form of psychological warfare, masquerading as a personal conversation.

Ironically, these chats can be made all the worse by your complicity and participation in them. The very fact that you are patiently listening, empathetically nodding your head while Mr. or Ms. Big Shot rambles on about your lack of priorities, thoughtlessness, lax work ethic, and failure to psychically anticipate his or her every need, merely reinforces their belief that all this is true. "We talked about this," is a phrase you will find comes back to haunt you again and again after one of these "let's clear the air" gabfests.

Even worse, though, is the situation that can arise with the emotionally needy boss. As we have tried to make clear, most Hollywood bosses are emotionally needy in some way. This can become particularly painful when the maltreated assistant is asked to assuage the guilt of the abuser. A perfect example of this happened to a twenty-four-year-old female assistant whose ogre of a boss summoned her into his office for a "little talk." The film *Swimming with Sharks* had just been screened and most of the office had seen it, but not the boss. "Come in, sit down, shut the door," said the ogre-boss. "What's this movie, *Swimming with Sharks*? Why does everyone keep telling me I should see it?" The assistant tried evasive tactics, "Well, Kevin Spacey's in it . . . and the director's new. . . ." But the boss would not let up. "What's it about?" he demanded to know. "It's about an assistant to an insanely abusive movie executive who finally strikes back by taking the exec hostage and torturing him." A long pause followed, then her boss asked, "What are you telling people? Are you telling people I'm one of those nightmare bosses? That I'm abusive? I'm not abusive, am I?" The assistant now found herself in the untenable situation of having to assure her boss that he was just the greatest guy and defend her own conversations with coworkers. "No, no, no. I would never say that. I'm so happy working for you."

This kind of twisted, classically codependent relationship can be found throughout Hollywood. What can be done? Well, for starters, try not to let your boss get too comfortable with his litany of complaints. Interrupt, sidetrack, try not to be alone in a room with him whenever possible. Be prepared for a "little talk" at all times. And by prepared, we mean ready with your agenda, your list of complaints and concerns. You may not get anywhere, but having the ability to derail the bosso-logue can save you painful capitulations. And remember, it's not "show friends," it's "show business."

Roll End Credits: The Recap

This is a wonderful business to waste time in. If you don't know what you're doing, you can wander around Hollywood for years, like a dog that's lost the scent, until you get clued in to what it is you have to do.
—David Dworski

One of the things you will quickly learn as an assistant is that you will need an outlet, someone to whom you can vent. You will need the kind of person who will really listen to you and the absurd details of your insane industry life. You can try talking to friends and family outside the industry, but even when you don't intend to bemoan your subordinate status, within five minutes you will inevitably become unhinged. Sometimes you will sound like a rude, vengeful, paranoid person like your boss, sometimes like a pleading child: "I'm just not cut out for it," sometimes arrogant and starry-eyed: "I am so in the thick of it, man!" Sometimes you'll just cry, and say, "It's all my fault."

The person across from you, or on the other end of the phone line, will be dazed and titillated, like a rubbernecker, amazed by the pileup of confusion you display: your heightened sense of important things happening, but not happening to you, your near mental collapse from such a rapid education, the contradictory impulses you project. They will see that you are a recipe consisting of one part "anything can happen if you make it happen" and one part self-loathing identity crash. They might not know how to respond to the chaos. They might say, "Well, what about that promotion you were talking about over Thanksgiving," which will depress you even further, since you were once hopeful, but now see nothing but vista upon vista of phone sheets and Post-its.

This is where assistant commiseration comes in, just like the camaraderie that exists in the worst boot camp. You'll need someone and you might be able to find him or her easily. There's always another basket case wandering an industry hallway somewhere, looking down at his shoes, wondering, What the hell am I doing? And you'll chat, over lunch at the commissary, in the brief exchange of a freshly xeroxed script, or in an aside during a conference call scheduling session that has been going on for three days. You'll chat and you'll give each other the assistant "nod," the look or comment that lets them know that you know. It's a wonderfully subtle pass of information. It's the way Jews communicated in Nazi-surveilled ghettos, it's the way drug dealers signal each other when a narc is in the mix, or the way a mother says, "Let the guest have the good slice." It's intimate, it cannot be spoken too loud. It has to be a whisper, because you're on the inside, outside the egos.

At a party where assistants dominate, you will find the kind of unraveling of tormented spirit and unleashed, trancelike drinking that existed in heretic witch villages of the Middle Ages. It's a real spew of stunted emotion, the kind that any prisoner dreams of: the one night off. Just one without the guards. And let's see what happens.

There is a class of assistants and because it's America, it is a movable class, not to say always upwardly mobile, but positioned for ascension. It's a gateway drug. A sip. So find your camaraderie when you need it, but also remember that it's not permanent, and some of the most successful players will tell you that they just plugged away, never embracing their status, always knowing this is not me, it's just me right now.

One hot, young manager, who was an assistant less than a year ago, and is now making six figures off of his fabulous roster of up-and-comers, offers the following advice: "Work really hard, but don't get too involved in the whole assistant hang. You know, going after work to all the assistant get-togethers at Le Colonial . . . keep a safe distance from the concept of 'assistant' because ultimately, you want out."

Everyone has a certain way to keep sane while hauling the same rock up the hill everyday. And when you're feeling like you'll never make it, you're not smart enough, you're not stupid enough, you're not tough enough, or you're not schmoozy enough, remember that Darryl Zanuck never even graduated from high school. Remember that David Geffen was an assistant, that your boss was probably an assistant too, maybe even just a year ago, and remember that part of the job description of "assistant" is to become someone who does not question, but obeys and fulfills.

From the scope of possibilities you are exposed to, you will chose your own path and you will fight and scream for whatever it is you believe in . . . but not now. Now, you are supposed to kiss ass and there *are* ways to do it with flair. You do it best by simply reaffirming your superior's sense of self-importance. As long as you believe that there is a life-and-death difference between Equal and Sweet'N Low, you will validate your boss. And most people who come to Hollywood to hold court are on a very simple search for validation. So do not indicate any sense that you find your boss's idiosyncrasies, ritualistic behavior, and weakness for every new fad that sweeps across the L.A. Basin in any way pathetic, or else you'll be considered precious and precious people do not get to make movies.

Surrender for this job. Surrender your ego, but also your time, your sleep, your life. Don't let it get to you, because even when you don't know that the nightmare is useful, it is. Navigating the pressures of being an assistant will prepare even the most shy among us for the world of making entertainment.

Whether you are a college graduate in a suit your mother

bought you at a discount rack right before the spring break interviews, or a lawyer with three years of practice under your belt, or a
forty-five-year-old divorcée starting a new life, if you have ambition, you will soon enough find yourself at the red velvet ropes
(granted, you'll be holding a clipboard and someone will be
screaming into your ear, "Are you on crack?! The agent who pack-
aged this movie isn't on the list, moron!"), but you will be there.
And you will find out that the expensive houses and lavish
lifestyles belong to people who, for the most part, engage in
pretty crappy, cockfighting battles everyday. And you'll learn,
maybe not immediately, but soon, what road it is that will take
you out of assistanthood. Maybe you do want the big bucks,
maybe you want to be the next Kubrick, maybe you want to swing
over to the tech side, maybe you just want to stay on the phone.
But whatever it is, an assistant job will point you toward it.

Nearby, no doubt, was Ava's assistant, ready to make all necessary arrangements. But imagine you were that assistant. Just for a
moment. If Ava didn't get out of there fast enough, you can damn
well bet, it was all your fault.

And remember, you're not alone. Things get tough for everyone in Hollywood, even the most glamorous movie stars. When a
press agent asked Ava Gardner, "Is there anything else we can get
for you while you're in town?" She responded, "Just get me out of
town, baby. Just get me outta here."